Gary Margolis writes important poems about important subjects, which he understands in emotional and intellectual depth, as *Seeing the Songs*, this fine book, now demonstrates in his lyrical prose.

—BILL MCKIBBEN
Eaarth: Making a Life on a Tough New Planet

Whether describing his intense time with Otavalo shamans in Ecuador, his journey through craters, playing ball with locals, or his adventures in the jungle with the Shuar people, Gary Margolis shares his experiences unashamedly, as if talking to his best friends.

"It is when we choose to see our fear that we go beyond ourselves in order to live the rest of our lives," Margolis writes. His quest for the elusive, yet palpable understanding of shamans is an inner and outer journey that requires courage and openness. His journey in understanding shamanic wisdom opens up possibilities to learn about himself and his particularly poetic view of the world.

—XIMENA MEJIA, PH.D.
Director of Counseling, Middlebury College

Gary Margolis has always been a poet, but in *Seeing the Songs*, he emerges as a Poet in the Emersonian sense: a Seer whose eyes are opened to the world and whose heart and mind sing back this wisdom in words. Moving gracefully through the re-dreamed jungles—both geographic and interior—of a journey to Ecuador and the re-membered communities of love that he found there, Margolis transforms memory into vision and vision into a call for action. He asks us to come to know and to protect these tribal cultures and sacred forests on their own terms, not ours. At the same time, with honesty and tender humor, Margolis invites us to face our own fears—as he faces his—and to heed our own sacred callings.

—REBECCA GOULD, PH.D.
*At Home in Nature: Modern Homesteading
and Spiritual Practice in America*

Gary Margolis masterfully describes both his inner and outer journeys as only an accomplished poet can do. He invites us to materialize our dreams, quell our nightmares, and experience life with indigenous teachers. *Seeing the Songs* IS being there. When you enter this incredible book, you enter a world where dreams and reality weave each other and "fact becomes poetry, poetry becomes fact." A brilliant book!

—JOHN PERKINS
Confessions of an Economic Hit Man

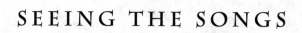

SEEING THE SONGS

SEEING
THE
SONGS

A POET'S JOURNEY TO
THE SHAMANS IN ECUADOR

GARY MARGOLIS

GREEN FRIGATE BOOKS
WINNIPEG, MANITOBA

ALSO BY GARY MARGOLIS

The Day We Still Stand Here

Falling Awake

Fire in the Orchard

Below the Falls

Seeing the Songs
First Edition, June 2012

Text copyright © 2012 by Gary Margolis
Author photo by Peter Lebenbaum
Design by Winslow Colwell/WColwell Design

Published in the United States by Green Frigate Books
417 Haney Street
Winnipeg, Manitoba
Canada R3R 0Y5
greenfrigatebooks.com/

The text of this publication was set in Minion.

ISBN: 978-1-927043-31-8
Library of Congress Control Number: 2012936614

By using a recycled paper, the environmental impact was reduced by 26,344 kg of landfill, 5,644 kg of CO_2 of greenhouse gases, 691,097 litres of water, 93,835 kWh of energy, and 42,809 kg of wood.

For Manos a Miazal,
for John Perkins,
who took us there,
for Daniel, who took us in,
and for my family,
who called me home.

Acknowledgments

The author wishes to express his gratitude to Middlebury College for supporting travel funds.

To Donna Stark and Linda Watson for encouragement and preparation of this book.

And always to my sister, Shelley, for her sustaining courage.

All author proceeds from sales and readings will support Waking Our World Community, sponsored by Dream Change.

www.dreamchange.org

CONTENTS

PREFACE

This is about fear—the experience and memory of fear—and the letting go of it. It is about how fear accumulated in my body and mind based on what I didn't do and what I had never done.

I begin by sharing the stories with which I grew up: of my father and uncles fighting the anti-Semitic bullies during the Depression in a Cleveland, Ohio neighborhood, of my father cold-cocking a drunk who cursed my mother, and of hearing my father threatening a man in a movie theater because he back-talked him when my father asked him to be quiet during the film.

This begins the moment I threw a stone from the Dean Road playground bench in Brookline, Massachusetts, and the stone skipped up and opened the shortstop's head. The bigger kid came after me with blood and fury. I ran away and had to tell my father that night after he came home from work—that same father.

This begins the day after college. I never had to go to Vietnam with my friends, and I never came home dead. Instead, I served a few ROTC months in San Antonio, Texas at Fort Sam Houston, where MASH units were made and flown away, where the burned were skin-grafted, and where some of the 1st Air Cavalry Huey pilots got drunk. That was where, one Sunday, I was ordered to watch a Dallas Cowboys' football game with a group of African army officers and explain the game to them.

This is about never training for the Peace Corps or learning enough of another language to say something useful. It is about never going so far away that I couldn't get back in the same long day. I only heard about my classmates who were trained, bused, and flown. Those who walked and rode horseback into the bush and had to sleep those first nights, weeks, and months with their terror and loneliness. Those who had to live with their feelings and use a language not their own.

This is about holding fear so long that it became me. It became the way I separated myself from experience, put fear between me and others, and let it become a substitute for doing things. The grandson of immigrants, I held my grandparents' escape and exile from Russia, their abandonment, and their fear of the new. I had learned to stay home.

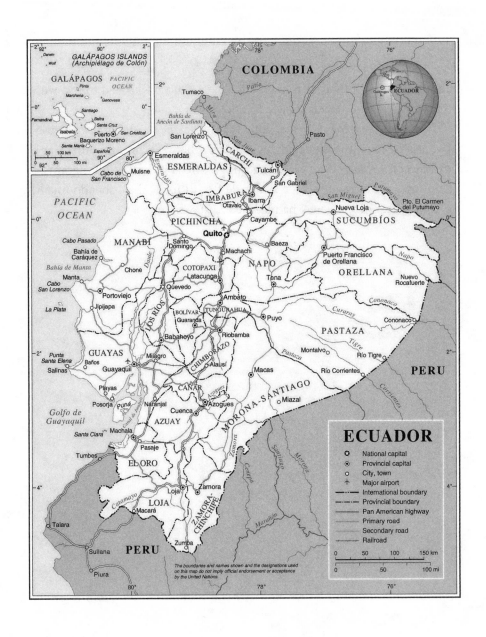

GALÁPAGOS ISLANDS
(Archipiélago de Colón)

GALÁPAGOS

PACIFIC
OCEAN

Darwin
Wolf
Pinta
Marchena
Genovesa
Fernandina
Santiago
Baltra
Santa Cruz
Isabela
Puerto
Baquerizo Moreno
San Cristóbal
Santa María
Española

0   50   100 km
0   50   100 mi

COLOMBIA

ECUADOR

Tumaco
Bahía de
Ancón de Sardinas
San Lorenzo
Pasto
Esmeraldas
Cabo de
San Francisco
Muisne
ESMERALDAS
Tulcán
CARCHI
San Gabriel

PACIFIC
OCEAN

IMBABURA
Otavalo
Ibarra
Cayambe
Nueva Loja
SUCUMBÍOS
Pto. El Carmen
del Putumayo

PICHINCHA
Quito
Santo
Domingo
Machachi
Baeza
NAPO
Puerto Francisco
de Orellana
ORELLANA
Nuevo
Rocafuerte

Cabo Pasado
MANABI
Bahía de
Caráquez
Chone
COTOPAXI
Latacunga
Tena
Nuevo
Rocafuerte

Bahía de Manta
Manta
Cabo
San Lorenzo
Portoviejo
Quevedo
La Plata
Jipijapa
LOS RIOS
BOLÍVAR
Guaranda
TUNGURAHUA
Ambato
Puyo
PASTAZA
Cononaco
Cononaco

Babahoyo
Riobamba
Montalvo
Río Tigre

Punta
Santa Elena
GUAYAS
Baños
Milagro
CHIMBORAZO
Alausí
Macas
Río Corrientes
PERU
Salinas
Guayaquil

Playas
CAÑAR
MORONA-SANTIAGO
Miazal

Posorja
Puná
Naranjal
Azogues
Cuenca

Golfo de
Guayaquil
AZUAY
Santa Clara
Machala
Pasaje
Tumbes
EL ORO
Loja
Zamora
LOJA
ZAMORA-
CHINCHIPE
Talara
Macará
Sullana
PERU
Zumba
Piura

The boundaries and names shown and the designations used
on this map do not imply official endorsement or acceptance
by the United Nations.

ECUADOR

⊛ National capital
◉ Provincial capital
○ City, town
✈ Major airport
   International boundary
   Provincial boundary
   Pan American highway
   Primary road
   Secondary road
   Railroad

0   50   100   150 km
0   50   100 mi

PART ONE
Spray Shaman, Candle Man

1

A NUMBER OF YEARS AGO, IN JULY, I RECEIVED A PHONE CALL FROM JOHN PERKINS, a Middlebury College classmate I hadn't seen or talked to in twenty-eight years. John said he was going to be near Middlebury, where I still lived and worked, and he asked if we could get together. We met and talked over lunch by the Otter Creek. I learned of his Peace Corps work in Ecuador in the late sixties with the Shuar and Canari Indians, and of his years in business and consulting. I learned of his world travel, studying and writing about how indigenous peoples view what we call stress, how they drum and psychonavigate, and how they mind travel.

John's life had been transformed by a Shuar shaman, who, on a subsequent journey back to Ecuador twenty years later, set him on a path he walks to this day. When John asked how he could repay the generosity of spirit he had received as a volunteer, the shaman, deep in the jungle at Miazal, replied, "All you have to do is change the dream and teach your children to dream new dreams."

With his Ecuadorian friend, Daniel, John has been bringing people to the Shuar—to learn from them; to help preserve the rainforest, indigenous culture, and livelihood; and to teach our children to dream new dreams.

John had recently sold his share in an alternative energy plant he and his partners had designed, and had written a four-hundred-page novel about the tensions between development and the environment in Ecuador. He was beginning again at mid-life to create a new focus and to take people to the equatorial rainforest so they could see and understand the depth of cultural, economic, and environmental forces there. He was doing this in the hope that they, too, would become committed to nothing less than saving the earth. John, I was to learn later, carried his own terrible misgivings about having, at one point in his life, helped "colonists" stake pieces of the jungle to homestead and graze the land with cows, consequently cutting down primary, unrecoverable rainforest. His new work was to recover himself.

This was a conversation and reunion I felt I had dreamed, that had been waiting in the wings of my life, and to which all my other days had brought me. Filled with feeling, image, and possibility, we reflected on the killing of plants, animals, and entire species. We were talking about beauty and, indirectly, what was lost in our own lives—and that we had never really known each other as freshmen in our college dormitory. We easily agreed, in that spirited hour, to stay in touch and to exchange our writing with one another. That winter I read John's book between my children's races at Vermont's Killington, Okemo, and Suicide Six ski areas. I read about politics, myth, and love in Ecuador's rainforest while sitting in their crowded lodges.

A year later, John, his wife, and their daughter spent an afternoon and evening with me and my family at Lake Dunmore, where my family was renting a cottage. It is a place not without its own stories of senior college students drinking and loving their days toward graduation. As we lay on a raft in the lake, John asked me if I would like to go to Ecuador with him. How easy it was to say "yes," days and miles away from that other continent, anchored and drifting nowhere, waiting for dinner on the shore. That night, on the screened-in porch, the bugs banging against the mesh, John told a story of camping in the jungle with vampire bats diving at his and the Shuar Indians' uncovered feet. John suggested they pull their blankets down for protection. They didn't and told him it wasn't their way.

Our hearts know when it's time to make changes, when it's time to transform a view and sense of ourselves. It is when we choose to see our fear and go beyond ourselves because we have to in order to live the rest of our lives. It is when we put something to rest to make room for our new selves and the purposes for which we are living. I had kept trying to resist the drama and melodrama of this psychological event, this opportunity. Yet, emotion voices the heroic in us. I suppose I needed to be aware of my fear in order to begin to re-create myself. In imagining going away, I risked going away forever, surrounding myself in the different, in things that could change me or kill me—things that could make me new.

In January, John and I agreed to invite a small group of friends concerned with conservation, spirit, and journey to travel to Ecuador's high peaks, rainforest, and Indians—to her shamans, her native healers. I said "yes" to this trip only half believing in my ability to actually go, yet already beginning to dream myself there.

2

IN 1959, I WAS A FRESHMAN AT BROOKLINE HIGH SCHOOL, AND MY GRADES HAD "slipped," as we used to say. Surrounded by four thousand other teenagers, half of them girls, I found it hard to remember what I had just read, harder still to compute formulas—the inevitable math block. With Sputnik newly orbiting Earth, schools were pushing numbers and the periodic chart like M&Ms, and I wasn't double-checking my work.

My parents and I decided to find a summer school that could teach me the habits of study. In New Hampshire we found New Hampton School, which helped me to find myself for the next three years. There I met Stuart, who became my fraternity brother, my best man, and my friend for almost half a century. Stuart wrote me letters while he was serving in Vietnam, some while he was on perimeter duty on the edges of Long Bihn base. It was his inflected "Good night, Gary" that I would hear next to me during my nights in Ecuador. I called Stuart at Deerfield Academy, where he counsels and teaches as a psychologist, and asked him to join us, not knowing that he, too, was looking for a mid-life journey.

I would never think of going to the jungle—or anywhere—without Peter, my Middlebury College and University of Buffalo classmate, neighbor, and dear friend. Brothers are sometimes made in blood. More often they are found in the shared pools of life's losses and celebrations.

Years before, we went hiking together ten miles out to a primitive campsite in Kejimkujik National Park in Nova Scotia. Once there, I felt myself coming down with a fever, my body's sweaty shorthand for anxiety. I told Peter I couldn't imagine being sick that far out. That is, I couldn't imagine surviving my own panic and my mother's warning: *Never be more than five minutes away from a doctor who makes house calls.*

Peter, constantly generous Peter, walked me ten miles home that night, back to our civilized tent in the park and back to my normal temperature. As we walked that trail, a buck bounded out in front of me. I yelled to Peter, who was bent over tying his boot and missed the only animal we would see on that trip. For that and everything else a lifelong friendship means, I called Peter to ask him to fly, bus, and paddle in Ecuador and to walk with me.

Peter agreed, and with the addition of Don, a newer Middlebury friend, our northern group was formed. We began to see ourselves first in our minds, away from our families and away in South America. Second, we saw ourselves in our bodies, building, over those winter months, shot by shot, the right antibodies for yellow fever, hepatitis, polio, and malaria.

3

THERE HAVE BEEN TRIPS I HAVE PLANNED AND CANCELED SIMPLY BECAUSE I WAS TOO rooted or too afraid to make them. That Wednesday, a mile from picking up Peter and Don to drive to the airport in Burlington, Vermont, I wept to my wife, "I don't want to say goodbye. Why am I leaving everything I love?"

The picture of my father driving me to the hospital for my first childhood surgery came to my mind, and I remembered his words, trying to tease me out of my fear: "Is this trip really necessary?" I remembered the initials with which he signed every letter he wrote to me when I was away from home at camp, at college, out in the world—CITKW: *Confidence is the key word.* My father couldn't stand fear and never put it between him and what he thought he had to do, so as a boy, he would fight. He fought without fear because he had to, because he had four older brothers who fought in the streets and a father who hit when he was drunk. Acting afraid was a shame that hurt more than being bloodied or bruised.

Yet my father, by virtue of the long hours he worked in the pool rooms and bowling alleys he owned in Boston, gave me time to grow up reading

and thinking in pictures and words. Although I could hit someone hard
on the football field, the idea of punching someone and being punched
turned me away, so I had never known if I could take or throw a punch.
I had never known what would happen to me or the other kid if there
was no one around to break it up. In that way, my fear and anger mixed
together. I had no periodic chart of those feelings on the wall to letter and
number that chemistry, those elements. I was half thinking this, feeling
terrified and excited, as we boarded Continental's commuter flight to New
Jersey, as we began to say goodbye to North America.

4

IN NEWARK WE WERE TO MEET STUART, WHO WAS FLYING IN FROM HARTFORD TO
join us. With time to kill while waiting for the shuttle bus to take us from
one terminal to the next, I made small talk with an older man—retired,
I thought—standing next to us with a woman I assumed was his wife. It
is easy for me to talk with people I don't know and whom I will never see
again. I combine curiosity and *chutzpah* with a need to make contact with
a stranger when I am feeling strange and alone. So we chatted. He wanted
to finish a roll of film and took our picture. I gave him my name and
address and asked him to send me a copy as a marker of the beginning of
our trip.

Strangely, he began cursing the rates in his hotel to the woman who
was with him, and then started telling us about sex in South America.
Fuck this and fuck that, he was yelling. A patent lawyer, angry and crazy
with the world, he was on his way to New Orleans. I had said "hello" and
given him my name. Peter and Don wondered if I was a lightning rod for
schizophrenics. They looked in the other direction.

On the bus, he said something to me that sounded half German and
half Yiddish. I heard the word *Jude*—Jew—and looked away, even though
I sensed he was Jewish. He resembled my uncles. He asked me if I was "one
of the tribe." I never said "yes" to his prodding, his attempt to bring me
into his persecuted mind.

Twice before in my life I had encountered my Judaism by confrontation. One afternoon at New Hampton School, during my first summer there, I returned to my shared attic room and saw a word I had never seen before—only heard. *Kike* was written on my desk blotter. I knew I was the only Jewish student in school there, and yet, growing up in a predominantly Jewish community, somehow I thought that slur was meant for someone else. I needed to deny that ignorance and hate, my anger and fear. Shaken, I found a teacher I could trust, Bert Lamb, and we walked the playing fields of that country school. That sweet Christian teacher taught me about anti-Semitism.

Years later, in Athens, Greece, my wife and I were treacherously sick with food poisoning. The night before, we had dined at a hillside restaurant and watched the light show on the Acropolis. We ate what we now think was unrefrigerated lamb. Cramping, vomiting, and dehydrated, we called for the hotel doctor. Hours later, a perspiring, seersuckered, balding man—Egyptian, he said—arrived from Piraeus. He picked up our colorful guidebook from the nightstand and asked, "Are your stools black like this or brown like this?" and in his next breath, "I knew a Jew once with a name like yours," and raised his eyebrows in my direction.

Was that a time to confirm my heritage, a time to bless my wife for keeping and using her given last name, Lynch? Was it a time to mumble something, pay his tripled house-call fee, and take his curative prescription? I've never known if it was the fear of saying "yes" to that Egyptian, his pills, or the tuna sandwich on white bread on our return flight home that turned my stomach right again.

I never said anything to that Newark inquisitor, knowing that he knew by my silence that he was right, and wondering as the door opened for us in front of American Airlines if he would send me the picture of us *kibitzing* in the New Jersey morning light.

5

BY LATE AFTERNOON WE WERE IN MIAMI, SITTING CROSS-LEGGED IN OUR NEW GROUP on the floor by the Quito departure gate. John, our leader, wanted the men from New England to meet the women from Florida and New York—Jane,

Macarena, Carolyn, and Nancy—and he wanted to instruct us on food, water, and money in Ecuador. Like students, patients, or good group members, all of us, at mid-life, knew how to go around a circle and say who we were, where we lived, who were our husbands, wives, and children, and why we thought we were going to Ecuador.

We boarded and began flying in a three-hour dream south.

6

AT NIGHT, QUITO WAS AN OCEAN OF LIGHTS, LONG AND WIDE WITHIN THE ANDES. After sixteen and a half hours of driving, busing, waiting, and flying, we landed. I took my first breath of thin air at over nine thousand feet. Past the Policia Nacional's passport checkpoint, Daniel called out, "Welcome to the Third World." Daniel, our Ecuadorian guide—six-foot-three, two hundred and forty pounds, black-bearded and long-haired—was a combination of Pavarotti, Che Guevara, and Tinker Bell. Father, brother, doctor, driver, teacher, friend, and bushwhacker, he filled each of the roles we needed over the next ten days.

Daniel's driver, Umberto, drove us through the empty streets of Quito to the Hotel Ambassador, where we paired into roommates that first night. How easy it was for me to choose my friend Peter, as if we were sophomores in college choosing to live with each other for a year. And yet, when we were both graduate students in Buffalo, New York, on the verge of renting an apartment together, I shied and never signed the lease. I was fearful that if we lived together, we might lose something necessary and nameless in our friendship. That night in Ecuador, even among other friends, there was no ambivalence to my choice. I wanted to hear Peter, friend to my wife and children, too, sleeping next to me in his bed; Peter, with whom I had shared my life, my fears.

I couldn't sleep. The combination of travel, exhaustion, and separation had me turning everything over in my mind, including the inevitable fear of not being able to fall asleep and of going crazy without sleep. I worried that I needed x number of hours of dreaming and sleeping each night, or else psychosis would cover me like the last plague to Egypt's first-born sons. It was so Western and North American to think I *had* to have a certain amount and that I couldn't miss a few hours of sleep. Peter was supposed to be the insomniac, yet there he was, sawing his wood for winter. I lay there seeing the image I had plagued myself with for months—a small bush plane taking off from the jungle floor and me standing there alone, without a quick way home. I played that film through my mind enough times to wear it out, thinking that a thousand previews would magically make the reality safe. I wanted to wake Peter, my unpaid therapist, who I knew would patiently listen and talk me through my fear. I didn't, the athlete in me wanting to tough it out, the healer inside searching for a releasing thought of peace and of letting go.

Amid the street noises and the chiming of the lobby clock, I picked out the engine of our room's—of Quito's—single-prop mosquito, whining in my ear. What was a mosquito doing here, high in the Andes? Was this the one carrying malaria? Did I need my head net yet? No matter where we were, this was to be the only mosquito I heard or saw in Ecuador. This was the whine of the divine distracting me until dawn, until the rooster crowed in the alley, and until I didn't have to wake up from the sleep I never slept.

7

AT BREAKFAST, EVERYONE LOOKED MORE AWAKE THAN I AND LESS CAUTIOUS, DRINKing the freshly squeezed juice. Seeing me pushing my eggs around the edge of my plate, Daniel said, "Go ahead, eat and drink. It's okay," an anthem he would repeat, with his pharmacy of pills to back him up. I would learn to eat in Ecuador and to be mildly sick along the way. Excusing myself, I walked to the lobby and out the Ambassador's door into the dry air. I wanted to see where I was and what I had never seen before.

Mountains surround and penetrate Quito, spilling green and wrinkled formations down into the streets. I thought of the *palis*—the valleys—I flew over a few years earlier with Stuart when he worked in Honolulu, another lush, volcanic place. We flew over the palis to what someone had told his wife, Nan, was the most spiritual place in the world: Kalaupapa, on the island of Molokai. We went to spend the day with the resident-survivors of Hansen's disease—leprosy. Our guide that day was Hyman Fujinaga, who had been exiled there forty years earlier as a teenager. As we prepared to fly back to Oahu, he said, "Do not forget us. We will still be here"—this voiced by a man who showed us an unforgettable hand-painted rock near the memorial to Sister Marianne, the missionary Father Damian's compatriot. On this healed and unhealed island, it read:

No Blame, No Shame.

I realized I was looking at and thinking about what I saw in terms of something else from the past, my urge to make the new familiar. Could I

see everything here for itself, on its own terms?

The buses were jammed with more people than could sit—going to work, or riding to some other part of that long city or further into the country. Many walked in this perfect light, compact and purposeful—Indian and white, women with babies wrapped onto their backs, men in jeans and suits, children dressed in the uniforms of their schools, and some wearing the felt hats of Otavalo. Everywhere color rose in their skin, in their clothes, and in the morning swirl of the city.

Overnight, Daniel exchanged the dented airport van for his custom-made truck. His company's new name was detailed on the side. The original name had to be changed because the rainbow in that word was too sacred to be used for business or to name anything else. The van, glassy and squat, was a combination school bus and plane, with six rows of two seats on either side of an aisle. Green hammocks could be secured on the roof for riding outside and for flying through the Andes.

Umberto, our sixty-year-old driver and surrogate grandfather, thin-haired and friendly, waited for us next to the van. We loaded our packs and plastic kegs of drinking water and headed off, first to change dollars into *sucres* (the inflated wad of bills our money became) and to pick up a detailed map of Ecuador from the only place we could, higher in the city at the Department of the Military. Next to the soldiers' checkpoint, a quartet of schoolboys kicked around a piece of folded cardboard, passing and scoring on one another.

Slowly, we crossed the street and kicked their ball with them, as if they were our sons and nephews. We tried out the few words in Spanish we knew. They played back, and as we were leaving they posed as a group, making Vs with their fingers behind each other's heads. We were parents and playful enough to play with all the kids we met in the Andes and in the jungle. More than once, what I'd learned as a child sustained me along the way—saying "hello" and "goodbye," "please" and "thank-you," as well as catching, kicking, and throwing a ball, and smiling because I felt like it and because I wanted to give back what I had been given.

We drove through the exhaust and noise of Quito, past its banks and restored Spanish "castles" and its monuments to workers. We passed a giant, sculpted hummingbird in the center of a traffic circle by the city's parks. We saw the Parque El Ejido, where recently twenty thousand Shuar and Quechua Indians had marched for days from the jungle, as warriors. They demonstrated and camped out, creating a people's park until the government agreed to honor the Indians' ownership of some of their own land.

Away from the traffic of Quito, we were on our way north to Otavalo, city of the great weavers, heading first to a small village where, later that afternoon, we came under the smoke and spray, spell and chant of the shaman, Teta Marcos.

Traffic thinned as we weaved into the mountains past hanging, curing pigs, past families waiting for buses by the side of the road and men peeing in the ditch, past gas stations where, Daniel said, gas was cheaper than Coca-Cola, and past mourners carrying their silver coffin. Everywhere we saw the terraced mountains and the local volcanoes.

Along the way, women with their babies and children shepherded their sheep and watched their cows. We stopped once to find a place to take too many pictures. We thought we wouldn't see another "scene" like this again, of a woman and her sheep. We had been admonished to sense when it was okay to click our shutters and when it was not.

Some Indians believed they were born through a hole in the sky and that taking their picture altered their image, their shape, and made it difficult or impossible to fit back through their birth hole to return to heaven when they died. Some simply didn't want to be used and walked away. One mother covered the face of her daughter when she felt a lens staring in her direction. Belief was a way of life and of living in and through this world.

What would I think, living on Sperry Road in Cornwall, Vermont, if one afternoon a group of travelers piled out of their van and took pictures of my wife and I, who thought we were alone, weeding in the garden and brushing the hair from our daughter's eyes? That first day in Ecuador I found myself trying to decide when to use my camera. I had some trepidation because I still carried a sting from taking a picture in my spring term poetry class. By luck, the Russian poet and filmmaker, Yevgeny Yevtushenko, was visiting the Middlebury campus and accepted an invitation to talk with my students about their writing. They brightened when he passionately said, "The worst thing is to say nothing and to be silent... Don't let your poems be a tight bale of hay or a wooden horse. Let the hay break open, so the dry flowers inside can fly." As the class ended, I took a few pictures of him talking with my students. Yevtushenko didn't mind, but some of my students were furious with me for becoming a tourist in front of them, making him, in that action, larger than he already was and turning myself into what one student said was an "ugly North American."

There, by the side of the road in Ecuador, my hands trembled holding my camera. Some of the pictures were blurred and some were untaken.

8

AT LAGO PABLO, DANIEL PULLED OFF TO A NEW RESTAURANT WHOSE WINDOWS looked out to a lake edging the terraced mountain, Imbabura. *There's almost too much beauty here*, I thought. I felt thrilled and guilty. I could drive through the *campesino* world with a Visa card in my pocket and eat grilled sea bass while watching a hummingbird farm its flower as the packed buses rumbled by and broke down on the roads.

This was our first meal together sitting around one table. The conversation was chatty and polite. I asked Daniel if he had ever been in the States. How many times during his nine years of guiding had he been asked, on the first day, "Have you ever been in my country?" by the French, the Swiss, and the North American *gringos*? Exhaling his cigarette smoke, Daniel said he had visited Ann Arbor and was on the verge of going to the University of Michigan when his father said he needed him to stay home and run the family hotel in Cuenca. So he stayed and studied in Ecuador. And then, taking us from surface to depth, he said he had been in Rochester, Minnesota, for consultation at the Mayo Clinic for a diagnosis he didn't disclose.

In anticipation of visiting the shaman that afternoon, we nervously talked about those native healers, the ways they cured and dispelled the demons, whether they used drugs—hallucinogens—and whether we would be expected to do the same. How quickly we came to one of my fears. Months before, I'd asked John the same question and had been reassured by his reply: "No one is obligated to smoke or drink anything he doesn't want to."

Years before in Buffalo, in graduate school with a woman I had just met, I took two long drags on a joint and immediately flew to the ceiling. I saw her quickly turn into a witch. With no prior tripping experience, I panicked and asked to leave her apartment. I asked her to walk with me to mine. I needed to flee the cauldron of her room. Outside, the wind was slanting off Lake Erie, and it was snowing. My fear changed to astonishment—did I change it?—as I saw each flake by itself. As the poet-priest Gerard Manley Hopkins had written that every hair of the head is "numbered," I saw each flake in its own diamond. Even after that night of kaleidoscopic light and love, the next day I was agitated, speedy, and not familiar with that chemical form of letting go. Here, even among friends, I scared myself about losing control. Yet wasn't this trip about seeing what needed to be relinquished in my life, transforming fear, and being in the world in a new way?

Daniel said he wasn't sure if it was his night of using *ayahuasca*—the vine of the soul, the jungle's visionary drink—that had eventually helped him and his wife conceive their children, or if it was his trip to the Mayo Clinic that had worked that magic. Perhaps it was both. This was a lot for a man to say so soon to a new group, especially because some of us were psychotherapists. My wife and I had waited four years to become pregnant. Either in Amherst, Massachusetts, at Stuart's house, the night before flying on a trip to Italy, or in Ostia-by-the Sea outside Rome, the god of infertility forgot to pass over our bed.

For years after studying with the poet James Wright one summer in Buffalo, when he was resisting his urge to drink, I carried with me some lines from his poem, *A Blessing*: "Just off the highway to Rochester, Minnesota/Twilight bounds softly forth from the grass...." The poem ends with the incredible set of lines, "Suddenly I realize/That if I stepped out of my body I would break/Into blossom." Wright, who eventually died of lung cancer, had been visiting his friend Robert Bly in Minnesota. They had been out walking after his diagnosis at the clinic when they encountered "those two Indian ponies."

After lunch, I recited Wright's poem to our group and to Daniel, an attempt at empathy and perhaps to go back into the safety of familiar words. Suddenly, I realized that if I stepped out of my body, I, too, could break into blossom. Through no coincidence, things were coinciding—memory and feeling, the past and the present, what I had dreamed and desired—image and word together.

9

IN MID-AFTERNOON, WE DROVE TO OTAVALO TO BE WITH THE SHAMAN. ON THE outskirts of town, Daniel had Umberto turn right down a dirt road, over its rocks and ruts, out to a group of adobe-walled houses, a village cast in the shadow of its spirit volcano.

I said "out," meaning *far away*, unconsciously to John when we were in the jungle later. I felt his anger at my use of that word. He had lived for three years in the jungle with the Canari, had gone through the depression and joy of living with them "there." He challenged my conception of where "out" was, what was "here" and what was "there." Where was my point of reference? He gave me a chance to revise my point of view.

Daniel stepped off the van first and walked into the small dirt court-yard to ask if the shaman was home and ready to receive us. After a few moments, he motioned to us, and we walked slowly into the yard. Two small, elderly women shelled and sorted maize on mats. Their dog slept up against the spread kernels. A child hid among their skirts. The stink of pig manure sweetened the air. From somewhere out of the adobe rooms, a one-hundred-and-three-year-old man shuffled toward us in his poncho, under his stained hat, and extended his hand in greeting.

Teta Marcos invited us to sit on a bench, a board balanced across two stumps, in front of the sacred room of his clinic, his chapel, his room of dreams and visions. He told Daniel he needed bread, flowers, fruit, tobacco, and *trago*, the strongest alcohol, for the healing ceremony. Daniel headed back to town and left us on our own for the first time. He assured us he would return.

The shaman asked Luce Maria, Maria of the Light, his great-grand-daughter, to take us back into the fields to pick bouquets of flowers and herbs for the healing and the ceremony. With her baby wrapped to her back, this beautiful Otavalan woman—gold-skinned, a blue and white wool hat pulled over her hair, traditional strands of gold seeds piled around her neck—led us through the backyards of her neighbors. We walked by their open rooms. Children played within sight of their mothers. A community water faucet dripped. We continued down a road to a path that took us into a small grove, blooming with little yellow flowers.

Jane walked and danced in front of me, blond Jane. In college, I was engaged to a blond Jane, who introduced me to poetry and who challenged me to keep our pet pig, O'Reilly, in my Middlebury dormitory room to prove my ability to be "spontaneous." She took me up the trail at Snake Mountain in Weybridge, Vermont, and showed me where to lie down among the rocks and flowers. She didn't return for our twenty-fifth class reunion.

We picked handfuls of flowers and followed Luce Maria, a twenty-two-year-old mother, back to Teta Marcos. She told us of her four children and husband. Daniel came back from shopping, and although something he bought wasn't exactly the right kind or enough—I think it was the whiskey—the shaman called us into his space anyway.

I walked into his dark, adobe room. My eyes tried to adjust to the candles lit in front of a Catholic-like altar. St. Francis held a skull. Against one wall, a day bed defined that darkness. Drying maize hung from the hand-hewn beams. Clothes, especially hats, and tools had their own nails from which to hang, like paintings bequeathed by a benefactor, never to be borrowed or moved.

Teta Marcos spread his mat in one corner. He carefully placed the breads and carnations, the apples and bananas in an ancient matrix. From a small, plastic supermarket bag, he took out his stones and other charms. One was a star he said he'd found, had found him, on a long walk many years ago. Luce Maria and her brother squatted to his left and assisted him, speaking in Quechua loudly, almost impatiently, so he could hear.

He asked Daniel who was there for a healing, and Jane and Macarena moved forward. John gave me his place in the front row of our semicircle. Mystery sat across from me in this wrinkled man I could smell, I could taste. I tried to edge away and shared more with John than I was prepared to share. Nervously, I asked him, "Are we going to have to use drugs as part

of this ceremony? If I'm sitting in front of him, can I step away after he's begun?" This was another way of saying, "Can I go home?" John wasn't sure, yet in his reply I heard his own anxiety. I stepped forward and took the unlit candle to rub its wax onto my skin and clothes. I lit the third candle on his mat.

The shaman handed out cigarettes, Marlboros, telling us with his hands to light the tobacco into smoke. I hadn't smoked in twenty years, but this wasn't about smoking; it was about sitting together with him and making breath and spirit visible. This wasn't about thinking of the things I had read of shamanism. This wasn't about watching myself entering into an experience. It was about being there.

Teta Marcos swigged the trago, and then with all of his hundred-and-three-year-old lungs, he sprayed everything before him—each of the sacred objects on the mat. And then he sprayed each of us, from right to left, as if we were his dry charms. I wanted to move back and to turn my head in such a way that I would appear not to be moving away. When was the last time I was spat on? Was it in my fraternity, Sigma Epsilon, one drunken sophomore night? Yet he really wasn't spitting so much as casting something out, over to us, and connecting us to him. He showered us with spirit, a spirited water with alcohol that we, and the Indians, have learned can disable and kill.

He chanted, invoking the other worlds, and moved his hands in front of his smoky face. After a while, he sensed our stiffness and, even sitting that close, our distance. Teta Marcos handed the bottle of whiskey around, motioning us to drink, saying he felt we needed to relax and become one group with him. So we sipped. As the bottle came to me, I tightened my lips. The images of my dead, alcoholic mother, grandfather, and uncle rose inside me. Was this the drug of which I was afraid? I had drunk little over the past ten years, but there, I wanted to taste and to enter in.

I drank, tasted the flavor, and felt the sting. With more chanting and smoking, spraying and sipping, and with an occasional swig of sweet Pepsi, the shaman was ready for his three participants to sit before him. I half watched Jane go first. I wanted to look at each of his objects and his totems in that room to see and take in what was there. I looked and waited. Then I took my turn in front of Teta Marcos.

I have been treated by doctors, listened to by therapists, adjusted by chiropractors, rubbed by masseuses, and blessed by rabbis. Here, I received what was translated to me as a "cleansing and balancing." Sitting in an old wooden chair, at 6'1", I looked into the eyes of this giant dwarf. Grunting and chanting, the shaman sprayed me with trago and washed the world from my clothes and skin. His great-grandson stood next to us holding a lit candle in one hand and in the other, behind the flame, a handful of

the herb we'd picked. With a powerful *whoosh*, Teta Marcos sprayed the booze through the flame, igniting the fuel and simultaneously the flowers. The boy jerked back from the blue fire and, shaking them out, handed the singed stalks to his mentor. Great-grandfather shaman rubbed the hot, smoking plants over my body. I felt the heat through my t-shirt and jeans and the ash on my skin. I smelled the burnt leaves in the air. After brushing me with these plants, he handed an orange to the boy, his apprentice, and again blew whiskey through the flame, igniting the fruit into fire.

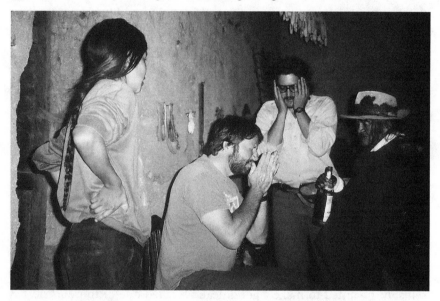

This time he placed the burnt orange on my wrist, inside my elbow, on my forehead and chest, and down to my hip and knee. With each placement, he growled and sucked powerfully through the orange, drawing into his mouth anything that needed to be cast out. With each "filling," he leaned to the door and spat, ridding himself and me of my demons and my impurities.

I looked at him and tried to engage his eyes. He was working hard and seemed uninterested in the "me" that wanted connection and recognition, wanted to pull him into the personal. He worked with and through something I couldn't see. Finished, I was told to close my eyes and then he took one last, gigantic mouthful of trago and sprayed me head-on in the face, gesturing for me to rub the spirit over my skin. I winced, opened my eyes, and was led to a corner of the room to wait while Macarena went through her ceremony.

Daniel had warned me to look away whenever the shaman sprayed me. Belief and ritual were woven into the fabric of the dirt, fire, and chant. Here I wore the poncho of experience, and under that covering I could quiet my self-consciousness and forgo analysis.

With the ceremonies over, Teta Marcos invited us to eat the bread and fruit with him—our communion—to take pictures and fold the petals of the flowers into paper to take with us. We thanked and paid him. I walked out into the new evening more confident and amazed. I had been washed with the drug by which too many of my family had died, in a place where, in James Wright's words, "Twilight bounds softly forth on the grass./And the eyes of those two Indian ponies/Darken with kindness."

10

IN THE ECUADORIAN TWILIGHT, WE STOPPED IN A VILLAGE OUTSIDE OF OTAVALO AT a weaver's house to see the gorgeous shirts and sweaters, belts and tapestries of those great craftsmen and women. "Bargain," Daniel said. "It's expected." Even with his permission, how could I argue $5—7,000 *sucres*—off a shirt that cost $8 and in the States would cost $25 or $30? Yet selfishly, I wanted to make a good deal. I wanted one of those intricately woven rugs with its brightly threaded fish and birds, swimming and flying in its stitching.

In one corner of the room an old man stood by his loom, gesturing to the women when he sensed one of us needed help. He was deaf and mute and was one of three *silencios* we would meet, each a guide for us in his own silent way. Quickly, the weaver's house filled with young girls holding their belts and scarves up to us. "Here, mister, take mine. Take this color," they pleaded. Their mothers stood in the doorway behind them, watching their salesgirls-in-training. Word must have spread that there were new shoppers in town. I stepped back into the van with a glow of pleasure and regret—a buyer's fate—at having something I wanted to take home to keep, yet leaving their pleading faces behind.

In the van again, the indefatigable Daniel said he had one more shaman in the outskirts of Otavalo for us to meet. The stars brightened. We passed a building with words painted across its face that read, "Death to gringos; gringos get out," which we were told was a demand to their government and not to individuals. Umberto drove us out of town, over the ravines of the dirt road and to another village, known as the Boston of shamanism, where other shamans came to learn, train, and be healed themselves.

The town was silent and secured. A few doors that were half-open closed as we drove by. Behind one, two men were cutting and sewing the felt hats that are the signature of Otavalo. We stopped. Daniel walked down the street ahead, disappeared for a minute, and then waved us to the entrance of a wooden, two-story house, the home of our second shaman.

We entered José Joaquin Pineda's home, part of a block neighborhood, and went across the wooden floor and up the stairs. "*Buenos noches*," his wife greeted us as we walked through their bedroom. (No one in Ecuador, as far as I could tell, passed by another person without offering a greeting, no matter who the person was or what work he or she did.) She had looped her twining from where she was sitting on her bed to a nail on the far wall and was weaving in extra threads to strengthen the thin rope, which would be used for commercial fishing. She challenged me to break a strand. Then I walked into the low-ceilinged, candlelit back room, past a small table set with Catholic icons and past a dividing curtain, where the shaman was sitting on his bench in front of his sacred work table.

Wherever I am, I have always needed to make a room private and personal, a sanctuary. As a boy, I walled my room with books, a soft- and hard-covered insulation. My wife, Wendy, has chided that I want to make each room into a reading room. It's true. When I walk into a room, like a dog curling into his safe spot, I look for a place where I can read, where I can feel safely alone. I think of that search as looking for a quiet place for thinking and daydreaming, a place to which I can go to leave the world for a while and be taken by that moment's trance in a book or a view out the window. I have the passion of a collector when I am in anybody else's private place, too. I look to see the things with which they have made their space sacred—beautiful and holy—for themselves, for their gods, and for their dreams.

I listened to José Joaquin introduce us to the beliefs and ways of his practice. I looked at his stones and totems laid on a cloth on his table—Shuar spear leaning in the corner, a picture of a local saint, herbs piled on the floor, small candles flickering in front of him, and his gold tooth and gold watch. Daniel and John translated his Spanish and his knowledge that things rarely happen without reason or without intent. He healed these intentional and unintentional spells and didn't cast them, unlike some other shamans. People came for their cures on their own and when medical doctors, stymied by their own failures and limitations, sent them. A teacher and a practitioner, he said much more, and helped us enter into the meaning and practice of his room, preparing us for his work.

From time to time, he took a drag from his cigarette and a swig of whiskey from a quart soda bottle and sprayed his stones. He seemed to be watering the charms in front of him, letting them know he was about to call on them.

He asked which of us wanted his work. Jane sat down and told him of her chronic disc problem from which, for a long time, she had been in almost constant pain. Dragging on his cigarette, José Joaquin slowly exhaled toward the candles on the bench in front of him with a whistle I had never heard and will never hear again. Half-flute, half-bird, he made the candles flicker with his smoky song. In that flickering, he read what the flames said.

Looking at Jane, he reported, "I can cure this. Some time ago, you stepped on a thorn that had been cursed with the dust of a dead person. This curse was meant for somebody else." Jane looked at him with relief

and gratitude. She replied, "I lived in Jamaica for seven years. Once, I did step on something that hurt. It punctured my skin. That must have been it." José Joaquin asked the rest of us to step back behind his curtain, so he could begin his work. Macarena stayed with Jane and whispered to us what she saw.

Jane stood in her underwear holding his spear for support. The shaman sprayed her completely with whiskey and patted her body with nettles and a bouquet of other herbs. Chilled, she shook. He chanted, whistled, and sang. Without her direction, she later said, he touched exactly the cursed and injured place in her back. He rubbed that spot with a cream and other things we couldn't see. He told her not to bathe for three days, what foods to avoid, and what herbs to use. He told her she was cured. Shaken, cold, and wide-eyed, Jane was pain-free and remained so throughout those days and beyond. How many healings have taken place when we have been forgiven by ourselves and someone else, when our pain has been released, taken over, or something from the earth has been applied?

I can't remember ever being told that a pain I was carrying was a curse not meant for me. I still can't say everything I witnessed or felt in the shaman's freeing explanation, that perfect forgiveness—a pain that was whistled and treated away, a belief we were invited to believe in, and a song half-bird, half-man.

11

WE DROVE AWAY THAT NIGHT TO A LATE DINNER AND BEDS AT A HACIENDA WHOSE tables were set for the rich. Washed and fed, I closed my eyes and fell into a dream I can't remember.

12

I WOKE UP THRILLED THAT I HAD SLEPT, HAVING LEFT MY FRETFULNESS IN MY BED IN Quito. The morning was clear and dry. The blue-green mountains shined, it appeared, with a light emanating from inside the landscape. I dressed and went down to breakfast, feeling the pleasure and embarrassment of being among tended gardens and saddled horses waiting for their riders. By the front gate, a girl walked her cow around a BMW parked outside the walls of the hacienda. I thought of my college's recent construction of a multi-million-dollar art center a mile away from the Vermont fields that used to graze cows. What was I going to do, seeing those simultaneities and feeling the harsh discrepancies—how beauty and politics coincide and how they separate and join us? It was easier to conceive of fear in terms of physical and emotional challenges—hiking through the jungle and traveling far from home. Yet the personal is also political, and what I saw pushed me to see one thing in terms of and *because* of another.

How are wealth and opportunity related to poverty and despair? What did I have to do to my own experience, my conscience, to see and feel both sides of these realities? What did I distort and deny in order to secure my place in the world? What would I do with my awareness? What was I willing to sacrifice to change my own attitudes and actions? What was I capable of feeling or seeing as part of, and not different from, myself? To what and to whom would I commit myself for the greater good?

My head buzzing, I sat down at the breakfast table. Jane sat across from me. After we had greeted each other and poured our coffee—a coffee as strong as syrup, mixed half-and-half with warm milk—she asked me if I

had ever done drugs or tripped. My heart blipped, adding an extra beat
to her question. How did she know what I was scared of? She said, in fact,
that she felt like she was tripping and seeing things in a heightened way.
She wondered if, having gone through my shamanic ceremony and having witnessed hers, I was feeling the same way she was. Suggestible and
anxious with her question, for a few minutes I thought I was tripping,
having somehow absorbed her experience—a contact high. *Listen to what
she said*, I thought. *She feels like she's high. You're not tripping.* I relaxed and
wondered if my fear was partly a wish or if I wanted to cut away my fear
of letting go in order to see everything that was here.

We delayed leaving for the market in Otavalo that morning. Don
had decided to wake up at six o'clock with Peter, Daniel, and John and
go back to the shaman's house so he could have an old shoulder pain
treated. I wandered through the flower and vegetable gardens, admiring
the thick, purple bougainvillea hanging from the wrought iron balconies.
I walked through the hacienda's library—the perfect study—wondering
which Indians had made the three masks hanging above the bay window.
Françoise, a college student from France who was bicycling through South
America and working there for a few months, pointed me to a weaver's
shop across the courtyard. I met Lucia, whose picture graced the cover of
the guidebook to Ecuador I carried and whose weavings held the stories
of her people and spirits in their woolen threads.

At ten o'clock, our van pulled through the gates of the driveway. Our
men returned as if they had been sailing all night to an island and then
caught the right wind to bring them back. They said the shaman we had
seen the night before had left for his other work, but they had found a
woman healer, a *curandera*, and her husband, who had performed Don's
ceremony. They'd told Don he was fortunate to be there; apparently, he
was in danger from an old family curse that needed dispelling.

I had never seen anyone with a beaming gaze like the one that emanated from Don that morning. He was entranced and smiling beatifically.
I don't know what he had seen in the healing ritual of that house. He told
us the details of the ceremony; Peter and John recalled those he couldn't
remember. I saw the ashes on his forehead, the small scratches on his back,
and the necklace of flowers he had been given. I felt the god he must have

seen without seeing anything. His gaze and presence were that strong. He was there and yet in another world. I knew him, and he was a stranger. I met my friend again for the first time. Beyond a few words of greeting, there was nothing else to say. It was more than enough to look at his face and to be with him.

A few days later, when the pain in his shoulder returned, I asked Don what he thought of the shaman's cure. "It wasn't about my body or the physical pain," he said. By noon we arrived, threaded and rewoven, at the market in Otavalo.

13

IN TOWN, DANIEL CAUTIONED US TO STAY IN SIGHT OF ONE ANOTHER AND TO BE aware of our cameras, packs, and the money in our pockets. He said no one would hurt us, but we could be freed from our things faster than Houdini could escape from his chains. Pickpockets in Ecuador are notoriously skillful at razoring a coin from a pair of pants.

We walked down the rows of stalls in the food market, past bags of seeds and grains, vegetables and fruits, and sheep heads, some skinned and some still covered in their woolly hides. Mothers sat behind their goods

chewing *coca*, a mildly narcotic leaf, and kept their eyes on their children. Many of them had been there since the middle of the night. Later in the afternoon, they would carry everything they had not sold back into the mountains, where they would refill their bags and prepare to return the next day.

Jane and Don hunted for the herbs their shamans had prescribed. The rest of us wove our way through the crowd toward the famous Otavalo square of weavers, stopping to put *sucres* into a blind man's hand and an amputee's pocket. One boy followed me, waiting for something to fall out of my wallet.

Riding a bus in Puerto Rico once, I was thrilled, like the other riders, when a local man entertained us with his perfect imitations of the calls of animals. He brought chickens, birds, an entire zoo out of the back of his throat. The Puerto Ricans took him casually. He must have been a familiar street celebrity, because they knew what he was going to do. For a finale, he vocalized a dog being hit by a car and sirens screaming in the streets. Some of us applauded as the bus slowed to its next stop. The man said something in Spanish that made everyone drop their heads into their laps and newspapers. He must have said, "You laughed. Now pay," because a few people handed him their change.

How could I pass these people I was taking in with my eyes and my camera without giving something back? How could I walk in the world in the same way again? What was I going to do with what I was seeing and feeling, and the realities I encountered?

As this was Friday, the day before the main market day, we walked through a quiet square. The craftsmen and women talked among themselves and attended to us when we asked about a price. Otavalans are known for their striking weaving—their brightly colored yarns, flawless knitting, and the images and stories threaded into their clothes and rugs. They are distinctive, too, in the beautiful decor of their clothes. They have been able to sustain their economy through their culture and craft, even as their nation struggles with a devastating international debt.

The women wore white blouses, dark skirts, and spools of gold seeds around their necks. The men dressed in white cotton pants and fresh white shirts. Everyone in this community and these mountains, including the children, wore felt hats. Everything at the equator was washed in a startling, direct light.

I searched for gifts for my son and daughter, my wife, my friends and office mates. Thinking about what I would like to give them made me miss them. I felt connected to each through the artful skill knitted into those Indian rugs and sweaters.

By two o'clock, loaded with hats, belts, pan pipes, and tapestries, we began our ride toward Cotopaxi, one of the highest active volcanoes on earth, and that night's beds. We drove higher and higher. I wasn't exactly short of breath, yet each time Daniel reported a new elevation on his altimeter, I drew in a shorter breath. Walking in different places, I did need to move slowly and not rush my steps or my breathing. I had to see more of where I was and the people I was among.

14

FROM TIME TO TIME, BETWEEN STOPS, I FELT OUR GROUP CATCH ITS BREATH AND TAKE its pulse. We used the time in the van to rest and talk in pairs and in fours, the thread of conversation sparking an idea or memory for one of us to share. We began to know each other the way teams and classes do, driving home after a game or a biology field trip.

Halfway to Cotopaxi, Umberto slowed and pulled over to the side of the road. I saw a small monument with letters and lines of a compass painted on it and under it, and in the concrete square, a large replica of the globe. "We are at the equator, the middle of the earth," Daniel said. Here at the world's green belt everything was itself, what my imagination could bring to it, what could be dreamt and sung about this place.

At the equator, I remembered how once I had wanted to see the place in Yucca Flats, Nevada, where the US government had tested its atomic bomb in 1951. I wanted to see for myself the first image on newsreel I had seen on television; I wanted to see the desert hole made by that radiating cloud, and to see if there was anything left of the houses and mannequins of Elm Street, the place the army had dummied up in order to measure the blast's effects on a "community."

I wrote the government and was eventually given permission to visit there with a small group of people who also had been given security clearance to drive out to ground zero. However, I never went. I don't know if, in making the arrangements to go and dreaming about the trip, I fulfilled my curiosity and need. I don't know if I was afraid to look into that hole, to imagine or hear a Geiger counter that still could be ticking. Yet here I was, in the middle of my life, where I said I wanted to be.

Umberto put the bus into gear. We pulled away from the cartographer's line. That place asked me to define a line and cross it to see the second half of my life—its necessities, its passions, its driving responsibilities.

15

WE DROVE FURTHER INTO THE ANDES, PAST THE NESTLÉ CHOCOLATE COMPANY'S main cattle farm and eventually to the town of Quinche, higher still. We stopped for a drink and a sandwich and to walk through the sanctuary of the Virgin of Quinche. Years ago, a girl had been cured there by a woman, since sanctified. The waters from the stone fountain are still drunk as a cure. The injured and ill arrive for their healing—walking, limping, and crawling over the square's stones and up the steps of the church. We walked through the vault of that shrine and read the testaments in words and pictures of those who had been healed. It was a testament of miracles. I continued to feel the blending of belief and dream mixed by the sun, an alchemical stir of transformation.

By the van, John and Stuart were fooling around with the kids in the square. It was a miracle how they made those dime-store tops spin in the dirt and onto the backs of their hands.

With daylight disappearing, we pushed on to see Cotopaxi before nightfall. We stopped for gas at a crossroads on the way to Guayaquil, the Pacific coast city, and saw two cultures—Ecuador's dilemma—the city and the countryside, mixed in the fumes of buses, in the farmers and oil workers jammed into those vehicles going one way and the other.

We continued winding our way through the Valley of the Volcanoes in the shadows of the mountains, which rose on our left and right. John and Daniel exchanged stories of the myths and histories of those peaks with the joy a detail can raise when it is remembered and added to a conversation. "Yes," Daniel said, "it's true, the greedy Governor of Macas was captured, and Chief Quirriba filled him with molten gold, making him 'eat his riches.'" Tired, we gathered our energies and rode over fatigue. The next new sight or story carried us forward.

John was ecstatic as we approached Cotopaxi and her snow-covered summit sparkled into view. A bit closer, we pulled over and got out to gaze at the shining volcano and her darkening lower slopes. John screamed and let out a whoop of joy as he was warmed by that sight in the chilly air. It was here in Ecuador that he felt most alive. It was hard not to be swept up in his passion.

With the sun setting, it was too late to ride up onto the volcano. We would have to wake up beside her. Umberto turned off the main road and drove through a corridor of giant eucalyptus trees that he said were the oldest in Ecuador; the ubiquitous eucalyptus, which robbed the country's topsoil of water and minerals due to its shallow root system. We arrived at the Hacienda Cuisine, an elegant former palace whose staff was preparing for a wedding the next day. Each room looked out to a courtyard of gardens and fountains. I worried that if I was found here, I would be made to drink boiling gold, too.

That night, Don and I shared a room. Before dinner, we talked about our wives and children and our mutual counseling work. I felt the powerful glow of his early morning shaman's healing. He was a man with a spell removed.

After a few beers—which at altitude feels like the hammer of a six-pack—we gathered around Daniel, who spread the large map he had bought in Quito on the floor. Two spines of the Andes stretched down Ecuador's back, the corridor through which we had driven. The vast territory of the Oriente spread to the east and to the jungle for which we were headed. The border with Peru was a dotted line that had been in dispute since 1942. This is a line of anguish and ambush, as there is still fighting there between the countries' soldiers and patriots among the Indians.

We asked about the Shuar, the Indians we would visit in the rainforest. Daniel began to respond and then hesitated. "It's better we talk about the Shuar when we are in the jungle," he counseled. "There you'll understand more." I felt my curiosity and anxiety rise.

Teaching us more about the geography and history of the land was Daniel's way of informing us about the tragedies of imposition his people bore: the burden of an impossible foreign debt, the discounting of Indian rights, the appetite and arrogance of North America and the West, and everywhere the pain of the disenchanted—people who had lost their dreams and myths. How quickly, in the comfort of the hacienda's parlor and the buzz of a beer, it was necessary for the talk of geography to turn into the talk of politics. As we began to express ourselves across the swaying bridge of our different personal and cultural histories, we were risking misunderstanding and disagreement. Yet even in our short time together, we began to create a sense of shared purpose, like a bowl whose clay sides could include its cracks as part of its beauty.

Hearing Daniel talk about injustice to people and destruction to land and to the human dream, it was clear that to deny or distort this truth would be a chosen sacrilege. This trip was about seeing things as they are and allowing perception to be personal, to feel and take personal responsibility for nothing less than the future of our planet, its environment and people. How strange and ironic that having "worked through" my issues of being the overly responsible caretaker in my alcohol-troubled family, I came to embrace my obligation to the earth and all of her people, plants, animals, and spirits—things I espoused and yet had only superficially embraced. I saw why I was in Ecuador, beyond and because of that sentiment and that necessary awareness.

At dinner, we tried to talk about our journey into the jungle, the rainforest, still a few days away, as if everything we knew was still unknown. I kept flying ahead between the images and feelings those words—rainforest and jungle—conjured, flying between fear and excitement. I kept seeing that small plane taking off and leaving me on the jungle floor with no quick way to get back to safety. I kept seeing myself swarmed by mosquitoes and bitten by what Alberto, a colleague of mine from Peru, called the green-eyed snake. "Watch out for that one," he had warned and teased me.

I tried to imagine the Shuar and the village at Miazal. John had described it as a few lodges in a clearing in the bush. I tried to place myself in a scene I had only read about or seen on film. When my fear approached panic, I tried conjuring the unnamed birds and flowers, their colors and calls. I wanted to preview what I had no way of knowing ahead of time, to control my fear by thinking, by seeing myself there and back home before I had actually gone. I was already back in Vermont before I slept in the rainforest.

Even with Daniel's reluctance to say anything about the jungle, there was too much anticipation among us to contain. John told us that the Shuar used to settle disputes by taking heads and shrinking them—*tsant-sas*—a tradition of honor the government had told the Indian Federation to outlaw. Shrinking the heads of sloths and monkeys became their ceremonial substitute, and I wondered when the last human head had been taken and shrunk. Someone nervously joked about the "shrinks" in our group. How had that term become applied to psychiatrists?

Quickly, the conversation turned to the Shuar we would meet at the lodge of the shaman Martin, Daniel's *compadre* in the jungle, and whether they used hallucinogens as part of their work. "Yes," Daniel said, "they do. If you want to experience that once we are there, I will have to send word ahead to see if that can be arranged. We will have to know for how many they should prepare the *ayahuasca*."

My stomach tightened. My palms sweated. With the flexibility of a stone, I blurted out, "Not for me, thanks." Freaking out in the jungle was the only picture I could project for myself. A few of my tablemates said the same. Others nodded to indicate their wish to drink. We began separating ourselves by this difference among us. Daniel sensed the tension and gently brought us back to the present. "You can always change your mind once we are there," he advised. "No need to worry. Here, have a piece of fruit." Daniel had an incredible way of helping us stay in the moment. *He's right*, I thought, *there's no need to worry now*.

After dinner, some of us gathered in Peter and Stuart's room, where John welcomed us to the world of psychonavigation, a practice he had learned from native healers in different parts of the world. He taught us that through imagination—opening to dream and spirit—we could engage our own animal spirits and travel to other places, where we could listen to what we needed to hear and see what we needed to be shown. I had done "visualization exercises" before in my therapeutic work. I believed in the power of living myth, yet there in Ecuador, psychonavigating, I saw the weeping willow in my front yard in Vermont. I felt her invitation to be swept by her branches and held in her roots.

All of us, including Umberto, quietly shared our experiences. I was grateful to have this grandfather among us. He traveled in his own dream, trying this way for the first time, letting his dream do the driving. Hearing those accounts, it was as if we had slept a whole night without sleeping. No, it wasn't "as if." We dreamt ourselves awake.

PART TWO

SMOKE IN THE MARKET, STARS IN THE CRATER

1

WE AWOKE AND BEGAN PACKING OUR VAN FOR THE DRIVE HIGHER INTO THE ANDES. That night, we would camp by the crater lake of the volcano, Tilipulo. Daniel and Umberto, with the help of Stuart and John, stood on the roof, rigging together a metal frame that would support back-to-back green canvas hammock-seats. Six of us could ride outside. An hour later, the bolts duct-taped in place, Daniel said goodbye to a friend who had driven in for a wedding, and we pulled away from the Hacienda Cuisine, down the corridor of giant eucalyptus.

I sat on one of the roof seats with Peter and Carolyn. We leaned against each other, the air our only seat belts. The bus bumped over the dirt roads. We swayed, ducking the low branches and power lines, stamping our feet and yelling to Umberto when we were afraid he had forgotten we were on top. "*Cuidado*—watch out," Stuart shouted from the other roof seat. We passed small farms—adobe houses with the families' crops planted nearby. A pig, chickens, and a few dogs ran through the corn stalks. People sitting outside, sorting corn, and hanging wash waved at us and at the surprise of our van and our roof-borne riders. Everyone returned our "*buenos dias.*" The words reached us through the road's dust.

Every inch of earth was used. The patterns of planting were ordained by centuries of culture and agriculture, a knowing how to live with that land. The mountains stood in the distance, green and brown, and we wound our way to them. Occasionally we passed through a town. People walked to market. In one village, a family shouldered its dead in a silver coffin. The elders and children walked in a parade of mourning to the crowded cemetery. Some of its graves stood above ground; swallows nested in its wall of white burial stones.

As we turned right toward the town of Puli, out of the corner of my eye, I saw a man or a creature I couldn't believe. He was dark-skinned, on crutches, and swirled in rags. His black, woolly head and face hair were matted. He walked as if he were dragging his body in a bag behind him, and moved as if he had climbed out of a hole in the ground or the rot of a tree trunk. I never saw anyone like him sleeping in a cardboard box on the streets of New York or looking out from a trailer off the road in the Green Mountains of Vermont. Was he a hermit, a wanderer, that corner's homeless, or—heaven forbid—a local Sasquatch harbored by the citizens of that town? I wanted someone else to see what I had seen. I shouted through the wind to Peter to look back. By the time he heard me, no one was there. There was no one to see. Were we too far away? Had he disappeared? What was it I had seen? As I did when I heard the birdman, the ventriloquist on the bus in San Juan, I felt haunted, held by the flicker of an image, the sight of a creature walking between worlds, between perception and fantasy.

We drove higher and higher into the Andes, up the one-and-a-half-lane road. We swerved to avoid an oncoming, overcrowded bus. Sheep and pigs were strapped to its roof. Umberto ground through his low gears, burning oil and brake fluid, as if the engine, too, reached for air at that new altitude—ten going to eleven thousand feet. Looking back over Cotopaxi province, the countryside was a geometry of squares and a floor of shadow and light. In my swaying seat, I was sitting on the wing of an airplane. A red-tailed hawk soared on the thermals. Usually afraid of heights and of riding out in the air, I flew through the mountains and out of my mind.

As we drove up and down the passes, seeing the Indians shepherding their flocks on the mountainside, John recounted his first days in Ecuador. He was a Peace Corps volunteer in 1970. Trained in business, he was sent into the jungle to "help" the Canari set up their local economy. After a long bus ride to Macas, he still had a five-hour ride by horse through the mud to Indanza, his village. After a few days there, he knew his skills were not needed. Depressed for months, John returned to Cuenca, where he could more readily apply his training. He never lost what he felt in the jungle. "All you need is your sleeping bag," John said. "A family will take you in and feed you as if you were a cousin."

Near noon and approaching Puli, we passed farmers and shepherds walking back into the mountains with their week's store of supplies on a burro's back and on their own. The brake fluid overheated as Umberto slowed around curves and into the crease in the hills that was Puli. A sharp edge of mountain, like a benevolent priest, overlooked the square and the surrounding plains. Here, high in South America, I felt as if I had climbed

Greece's Mount Parnassus to Delphi and the Temple of Apollo. I believed Apollo, the sun god, was born in this bowl, too.

We stepped out of the van and into another world. Lamb and chicken were being boiled and fried. Vegetables and fruit lay on folding tables. A few seamstresses, sitting in a row, sewed hats. Most of the goods—boots, t-shirts, and flashlights—seemed to have spilled out of a bus driving through the mountains. Indeed, a salesman stood on his pickup's tailgate and shouted into a scratchy mike, hawking his tapes. Dogs picked among the lunch bones and banana skins. Children held onto their mothers, who were stirring the soups. Some slept and played under their skirts. A few men lay dead drunk in the road.

I walked down the rows inside the cooking smoke. I didn't know where I really was, lost and dizzy among friends and among the sweetly unfamiliar. All I could do was be here. There was no other place to go or to return to. Like a child, I could only look and listen, say "please" and "thank-you," and trust what there was to trust. Through the haze, I heard Daniel say, "Gary, sit down. Eat. Drink some soup."

I gulped air, fearful that anything I drank or ate would make me sick. How could I refuse the chicken soup and the boiled corn on the cob? When was the last time I didn't eat with such an invitation? So I sipped without swallowing and chewed without eating. A few men crowded around us. Women, sitting in sets of threes and fours on their balconies, looked in our direction. Two British college girls sat on the curb, waiting for a bus to take them back to Quito. Everyone was held, suspended, in the market's dust and smoke and that afternoon's dream.

Umberto honked, and I climbed back into the roof hammock. I wanted to ride outside. I wasn't ready to be part of a conversation or to say what I was thinking. I wasn't lying in a hotel bed or ordering sea bass and looking through the bay window at Lago Pablo. This was different from browsing through my stack of CDs and slipping one into the player for the ride home from work, or sorting through my closet for my best dress shirt.

We left Puli, driving around a man lying drunk or dead in the street. Going north, the dirt road was just wider than a bus. "This is the old Pan American highway," John shouted to me through the wind. "I don't know why, but years ago, at night, the drivers used to shut off their lights when they came upon another bus." *Because they drive blindfolded*, I thought.

The kids we passed shouted for gifts upon seeing a strange van, knowing there were *gringos* with things in their packs to give away and leave behind. The dust on that ride was a meal. The afternoon light lengthening on the mountains was a changing painting. What would it have been like to stay here, to be at the end of a long horseback ride beginning a two-year tour in the Peace Corps or opening the door to another life?

2

BY DUSK, WE ARRIVED AT THE RIM OF QUILOTOA, WHERE WE WOULD CAMP FOR THE night down in the crater. At twelve thousand feet, I walked in the lead boots of a deep-sea diver. Our van was surrounded by kids. On a knoll nearby, their parents sat wrapped in wind and their woolen ponchos. Their bright acrylic paintings were spread out for sale in front of them—scenes of their lives and countryside painted on stretched llama hides. One man, away from this group, strummed his autoharp. A boy next to him fingered a stringless guitar. I found a place in my pack for a hand-sized painting. It vibrated like a drum when I played it with my fist, an instrument my son could beat in his room.

Back at the shrine, we wondered why Daniel had searched for hot water

to fill one of the large plastic kegs. "Tea or coffee, anyone?" he asked, as the Indians and Quechuas strapped baskets holding our food and tents onto their backs for the hike into the crater. I had kept the sense of safari sufficiently at bay. Even knowing these men would be paid well for their work, seeing one of them carrying a case of Pepsi, I felt embarrassed and distant from him. In fact, they were part-time sherpas and could walk the narrow, stony paths in their sleep. Short, barrel-chested, and bronzed by the sun, they herded and farmed on those grassy slopes.

I slipped on my pack and walked to the crater's edge. Hundreds of feet below, the still, slate-colored lake barely riffled in its bowl. The water was held in a breathless brush stroke. I could fall or fly. I was afraid to keep looking, fearful I would step out onto the wing of the air. Leaning, I stepped back and joined the others to begin the trek down.

We walked and slid. The Quechua men and their sons ran their pan flutes across their lips. The breathy, hollow notes floated down like feathers. No one, luckily, twisted an ankle. Seeing sheep herded into their pens across the mountainside steadied our steps. If it had rained, a few of us could have slipped into the shelter of a nearby shepherd's hut. Its branches bent over next to the trail, a refuge in which the poet-monk, Thomas Merton, would have loved to sit in meditation.

As the sun inched down behind the rim of the crater, we reached the shore of the lake. Looking back up at the rocks, the trees, and the walls of the bowl, I knew I was here for the night. And for some reason, by this time, I felt no panic, no need to retreat or think I needed an instant way out. I looked across the effortless water a half-mile or so to the other side. I smelled the volcanic mineral as if I were at the edge of a sea. From nowhere, two burros trotted down to the water to lick the salty stones, their rope leads trailing behind them.

No hacienda here, we spread our nylon tents and their maze of poles and made camp. Rolling out my bedroll, I felt a summer-camp twinge of tension. Who would be my tentmate? How would we decide? We were men and women held by no college's rules. Stuart and I, in the comfort of our long friendship, asked each other to share the red tent. We graded out the rocks with our hands. Umberto and Daniel hooked up the gas grill for boiling water and frying vegetables and beans. A few Quechua walked onto the trail and carried back loads of branches for a fire, enough for a football team's Friday night bonfire. Don knelt with one of the men, showing him how to juggle—first one ball, then two, then three. Both laughed with each success and failure.

With the light changing quickly, the Quechua sat in a semicircle playing their flutes and drums. The notes fell into a melody like a half-remembered dream. I wanted to be with myself and walked to a spit of rocks edging out into the water. I sat down, crossed my legs, and breathed the breaths of meditation. I thought about being here in a crater at the equator. The earth's fire flamed deeply beneath me. I felt the deep con-

nection to everyone I loved and whose love had touched me. Slowly I
brought to mind and to heart each person—my family, neighbors, friends,
and co-workers—with whom I had shared my life. Love rose through the
ground, through my body, and out through my mouth and eyes. I released
and shared it, sending it to my campmates. I beamed it across the world. I
heard John Lennon sing "All you need is love."

Empty and filled, I rejoined the others and the happy chant of their
song. Jane danced and shook her cow hoof rattles and maracas. Before
long, we were all dancing and weaving ourselves among the tents and
musicians. I don't know how those Indians came to be playing for and
with us. Did Daniel ask them to bring their instruments? Did they do that
on their own? In that song and dance, there was mutual delight. As the
sun set, they used what light was left to climb up the canyon, although, no
doubt, they could walk it in their sleep.

One of us thought of a way to give back what we could. We stood in our
new choir, in that crater, and sang *Amazing Grace* to them as they prepared
to leave. Their leader's eyes misted. He bowed his head. We had graced
each other in our human exchange.

The Quechua would return the next morning. As we ate later that evening, we heard a few flute notes drifting down like a hand waving, or a voice saying "good night."

After dinner, we lit the dry, gathered branches and for a few hours, stood and sat around the fire talking and looking into it. Peter was its main tender, bringing more wood as we needed light and heat. Occasionally a shepherd's dog barked in the far darkness. We talked quietly under the canopy of stars and constellations that most of us had never seen in this hemisphere before. The Southern Cross hung like a sword.

In front of a fire, a summer camper at heart, I suggested we make a poem by going around the circle, each of us adding a line that wanted to speak. In the stillness, I said, "By the crater's lake, only a dog sings…" The poem emerged like a dream of the group, image by image, feeling by feeling, until it reached me again and its inevitable refrain became "Because, by the crater's lake, only a dog sings."

As the fire died, I walked beyond our tents and sat down in the darkness. In those days and nights in Ecuador, I tried to resist seeing myself in someone else's words and in something I had read. I tried to feel a common spirit, and our points of intersection. If Narcissus looked in the night mirror of this lake, he would see the stars and not himself. Sitting here, I grew out of the dirt and was rooted in it. Held in my body and released through breath, I was a stone, a small bush, and the air.

After a few minutes or hours, I walked back to the tent I shared with Stuart, unzipped my nylon mummy bag, and crawled in. For years—I don't remember how it began—whenever we shared a room together, Stuart and I had said a round of teasing "good nights." We wanted to happily annoy each other and hit this farewell back and forth like a tennis ball. "Good night, Stuart," I would say. "Good night, Gary," he would reply. And on and on, until one of us fell asleep and hit the ball into the net.

In the cocoons of that tent and that bag, I didn't know whether I was awake or sleeping, thinking or dreaming. The air was cool and bright. I tossed and turned inside the crater, inside that sleepless dream.

3

I WOKE UP OR DREAMT IT WAS TIME TO UNZIP MY SLEEPING BAG. THE OTHERS STIRRED in their tents. Daniel coughed, clearing his chest of smoke. Outside, the sun hadn't broken the rim of the crater, even though dawn had come and gone. Someone chuckled, and then, in Spanish and English, a voice reported that dogs had scavenged our unstored food and our breakfast. Those were the dogs, bold as raccoons, we'd heard barking and howling in the distance.

The sun edged up and filled the lake with light. Suddenly a string of burros pounded down the trail and trotted to the water to lick the salty stones. The band of Quechua appeared, the leader with his wife and the others with their sons. José looked puffy and tired and said that in celebration of our singing together, his men had stayed up all night drinking. He also said that they had been sick after painting a house the day before. Daniel asked him about their paint, which he thought was made with lead, causing their nausea and dripping eyes. He told them that on his next visit he would bring them safe, unleaded paint. Wherever we were, Daniel talked with the Indians in friendship as their *compadre* to learn how he could be of support to them.

The kids hung around us as we broke down the tents and repacked our things. They put out their hands for an empty film canister, a pen, or anything they could use or make into a toy. I had a pad of writing paper. I sketched, in simple lines, the lake and surrounding hills. A five- or six-year-old boy sat next to me in his felt hat, poncho, and rubber boots. When I handed him the paper, he copied my drawing exactly and signed his name at the bottom. I gave him my pen and a few sheets of paper. His father, sitting nearby, gestured for me to hand him the whole pad. I did, feeling guilty and happy in that small, prodded relinquishment.

The burros came for us. To hike that canyon at that altitude and pitch would have taken all morning, if, indeed, each of us could have made it. Daniel had brought cylinders of oxygen, but we hadn't needed to use them yet. This was no place for any of us to be taking our first, unmonitored stress test. The Quechua put blankets on the burros, tied on rope halters and reins, and boosted each of us onto a burro. Next to me, Nancy cried. This wasn't her desk in New York City. She felt terrified of the ride up the stony path, never having ridden before. It was hard for any of us to know when a personal fear would emerge, or when the only thing to do was what needed to be done next. We could say "I don't want to. I can't." And yet, time and time again, we did what we couldn't do and what we had never done before, with the courage of a man or a woman and with the determination of a donkey. Nancy was afraid of falling and of dying. She said this directly. I was only one fear away from hers. My terror was cast in the days in front of me. I said, "Nancy, the burro has climbed these paths a thousand times. His driver will lead you. You don't have to do anything to make him walk safely."

She gathered herself—as she would a few days later in the jungle—and rocked and rode, urging herself to the top. The Indians climbed next to us as if they were walking on a level road. They kept those braying burros to their task. Six feet tall, my feet dragged in the dirt. I was sure this creature would cave in. Up the trail, Carolyn sang a few songs I remembered from grade school. For an hour we switchbacked our way to the top. The lake and its crater filled in behind us. Fear dissolved in the crystal air.

Near the rim, the rocks formed a tunnel. We passed a shepherdess bringing her flock down to graze for the day. Her sheep and dogs swarmed

around us, a woolly tide. We greeted each other in that traffic, each going our own way.

Umberto pulled the van up to be loaded. The villagers were back with their paintings and the kids, again, asked for prizes. I handed out some of the pink rubber balls I had brought from home. A man came over holding his smallest son and said, "*Por favor*, please give something to him." I had a jar of bubbles and a few plastic pipes, which I saved for the youngest children I met. I gave the boy one of these.

Slow to leave that place because of the feelings among us, we were thrilled when the men invited us to a few games of volleyball. Their dirt court was nearby and their ball in hand. The invitation turned into a playful challenge—two out of three games with twenty bucks to the winners. They played three-man teams and couldn't understand why we needed all five of us. A few of their friends jokingly joined them to mirror our side. A volleyball match at eleven thousand feet!

Daniel and Macarena translated the score. The children squirmed in the hammocks on the roof of our van and shouted "Viva Quechuas!" Our size and unearned cockiness meant nothing and rarely converted into points. I had never seen a net set so high or held a ball this heavy. They crushed us, running into perfect formations against their plodding opponents. In two games, we scored four points. We lost our money and our breath. What a joyous defeat. Of course, for days we replayed the match and boasted about what we could have done at a lower elevation. No way. They would have beaten us anywhere in the world.

After another round of picture-taking, we sadly stepped into the van and drove away. The boy who had followed me since I gave away the balls ran behind us. He yelled, "*Señor, señor!*" He knew I had more left. He knew I would give in as if he were my son. I threw a ball into the growing distance between us, happy to have nothing left to give away.

We backtracked our route down through the mountains on our way to Baños, city of the famous thermal baths. There we would cross the Andes to the town of Shell and fly into the jungle to the Mission at Miazal. Umberto forgot we were riding on the roof. Bumping and swerving, the van seemed to drive itself as we dropped through these elevations. Peter, Carolyn, and I huddled together in our sky seat. "I'm sitting between my brothers," she said, burrowing under her poncho away from the dust. Occasionally we passed another bus on its way to Puli. I tried to doze away the sleep I lost in the crater. Rest was in the view in front of me in the mountains. My dream was in the ride.

John wanted us to explore the abandoned hacienda we had passed the day before. It was the place he and Daniel hoped they could turn into a learning center for students studying Spanish, the ecology of the rainforest, its Indians, and Ecuadorian culture. Two girls, caretakers from Tilipulo, let us in through the gate. For an hour we walked through the empty, vaulted rooms, chambers for the echoes of what had been said here. "A poet could read her poems to the moon in this place," Daniel said. This was a house for romance and ghosts.

Gardens bloomed through the ruin. Time passed on a sundial in the courtyard. A large, ancient urn held rain. Absence and neglect would eventually crumble the walls and hand-blown glass windows. The city needed to sell these buildings for a song and indeed, singing, money, and commitment were necessary for saving and restoring this place. Desire and necessity needed to merge into purpose.

I felt John and Daniel's passion for joining the political and poetic, the just and the beautiful. I knew I was there for reasons personal and universal—to save myself, to save nothing less than the earth, and to rededicate my life. I feared saying anything like that to myself, wanting to keep separate from a "movement," an ecological "jargon." But that was just prideful, a false superiority and a lack of focus. I saw and felt what could occur there—the restoration of a building for a learning center. Moreover, I had to acknowledge what needed to be changed where I lived in the North, in my own heart, and in my own dreaming. In the spirit of our group, too, energy grew that wanted to define and direct itself into commitment. What on this "working vacation" did I need to vacate, to empty myself of or let go to ruin, so something else could rise and could work in me?

Stepping into the van, Umberto asked us to help him dismantle the roof seats. We were about to drive through towns and cities, and he was afraid we would hit the power lines. We climbed back inside to our two-seated rows like children riding home from school. In Latacunga, in mid-afternoon, we stopped for lunch. Daniel said a few pills from his traveling *farmacia* would stop the runs. "If you get sick," he cautioned, "come to me. Don't take those medicines you brought with you. They don't let the sickness run its course and be over." How easily I let go of my mother's admonishment to always check a doctor's degrees on his office walls. Daniel was the doctor. He had the cure.

We drove down through the changing foliage to Baños. The air became moist, heavy, and more breathable for us flatlanders, even at three thousand feet. I thought of Worth Mountain and the Middlebury College Snow Bowl where I lagged behind my children, skiing at a thousand feet in the Green Mountains, almost level compared to these Andes.

The valleys opened before us. The vegetation changed into flowers and fruit as we approached this side of the rainforest. Near Baños, Daniel pointed to the left and said, "Here's where the big earthquake buried those towns. Everything was lost. Thousands of people were killed. You can see the rebuilding." I thought of the time I felt my own house shake during an earthquake. The glasses rang against each other when the earth shuddered from an epicenter a hundred miles away in the Adirondack Mountains. In Ecuador, along this spine of mountains, the earth is still shifting. The people live in a fearless fear. In 1987, parts of Quito shook and crumbled. The world sent aid to that burial ground. The gods are still young and passionate here. The earth still splits apart.

When I'd picked up the forms for my passport at the Addison County Courthouse in Vermont, I had read the list of countries about which the government advised, "Travel to only if necessary." I worried about terrorists and disease, not earthquakes. Living where the ground opens and the mountains smoke has taught the residents of Ecuador to live with the natural reality that the earth has its own way. I thought of the Alcoholics Anonymous bumper sticker, "Let Go and Let God," which in Ecuador could read, "Let Go and Let the Gods." Daniel had learned not to obsess about the future. He knew how to be where he was. He could help us untie the knots of fear we fed our minds.

When we reached Baños at six o'clock, the streets were filled with shoppers and strollers. Girls walked arm in arm. Families bought things with their eyes, standing in front of the store windows. Music poured from doorways and cars. The vendors had their racks on the sidewalks—shirts and sweaters, the city's bright flags. People came to Baños from all over the country and the world for the soft light and air and for the hot, healing mineral baths.

We checked in briefly at our hotel. The stores were closing, and we had to buy the rubber boots we would need the next day when we walked in the mud in the jungle. I wouldn't wish nine *gringos* trying on boots, sized in metric, on any storekeeper no matter how many *sucres* they paid. The local people smiled as they walked by us, as we jammed our feet into the boots. Daniel and I were nearly the same height and weight, and he told me they didn't make boots in our size in Ecuador. "No size twelve. Don't worry," he said, "I'll have a pair for you in the jungle."

Back in our small hotel room, Stuart felt feverish and frustrated with getting-sick-when-you-least-want-to. He said he was used to becoming ill when he let down and when he went on vacation. After eating a little rice and water, he went to bed early. Sitting in the lounge before dinner, more of us took pills. John said that sometimes he had seen people getting sick because of what they expected to happen—being too careful about water and food. It was hard to believe that diarrhea could be psychosomatic. Yet there is a link between what we think, how we feel, and what our bodies make of us.

At dinner, Daniel introduced us to Lucho, a friendly young man who would cook for us in Miazal. *A cook*, I thought. *When are we going to really rough it?* Again, the conversation turned to the jungle and the Shuar. As usual, Daniel found a gentle way to keep us, for now, in Baños. "It's better to speak of those things there, where they will make more sense," he said. He did remind us that we should try to decide whether or not we wanted to take the *ayahuasca*, so Martin would know how much to prepare.

I thought perhaps I would drink it after all, surprising myself. I realized I felt less afraid. I imagined things differently. I saw myself in a wider realm of possibility. At any rate, I didn't have to decide then. I could sleep in a dream of *perhaps*.

I went back to our room to pack the things I would need in the jungle. "Take only the minimum, the absolute minimum," Daniel warned. He was familiar with the small plane we would load and with the hike into the rainforest.

Stuart slept, sweating out his fever. I went through my things as if I were folding a parachute. The reality of going into the jungle was at hand. Would I need one shirt or two? Would one book be enough? Which one? Could I survive if I didn't have a library of books to read? I was doing what I had said I was going to do, and what I had imagined doing months before. I worried about dying, but the real question was *how was I going to live*? To what values and practices did I need to commit myself? These were the questions I kept asking the year—and the night—before I flew into the rainforest. Packed and repacked, I climbed into bed and looked out the open window. Was that the moonlight or the waterfall cascading down Tungurahua's steep hillside?

PART THREE

RIVER IN THE FIRE SINGING, UNCUTTING THE TREES

1

AT DINNER THAT NIGHT, A FEW OF US HAD DECIDED TO MEET DANIEL AND UMBERTO the next day at six a.m. to drive to the thermal baths before breakfast. A fine rain fell as we drove through the cobbled streets of Baños, past the town soccer field and wooden, white-towered church. Six pilgrims had arrived early, before the crowds filled the entrance to the mineral pools. We paid our *sucres*, stripped down to our bathing suits, and walked in the steamy mist down the broken steps to the tanks, thick with sulfur. Yellowish and over a hundred degrees, the water poured out of the heart of the mountain. The elderly and disabled bathed at this hour. They greeted us with nods and a few instructions, and showed us where to sit to feel the full effect of the volcanic spout and the nearby stream that would cool us. One woman disappeared into the healing soup and swam underneath, head-first into the shower. She surfaced next to me, smiling and flushed. When an Indian walked in naked, she was quickly told to cover herself by the attendant. We felt as anonymous as patients in a clinic. A half-hour later, clean and perhaps more healed, we climbed into the van.

Back at the hotel, we stored all the things we wouldn't need in the jungle in one room. With more of us sick, Daniel needed to return to town to replenish his store of medications. We waited in the parking lot and killed time with the patience of travelers waiting at their gate for a late flight. Carolyn did her morning form of Tai Chi. Stuart and I walked around the streets. Each of us anxiously pictured the flight into the jungle.

Months ago, when John suggested we travel to Ecuador, it was the words "rainforest" and "jungle" that tapped my feelings. I was flooded with pictures from magazines and movies, most of them beautiful and none of them safe. I saw leopards, snakes, and vines, cities of insects, parrots and monkeys, walls of flowers, and flesh-eating Indians. Most of what I imagined was nameless. Everything was remote. And much was disappearing, cut, burned, and made homeless. I tempered my fear by using both sets of words—rainforest and jungle, flowers and snakes. I saw myself bitten and stung, yet also held and protected by the twining vines, bird songs, and things I had never heard or seen and would probably never see again. Each word held a part of me, yet I had to remember, beyond images and words, that what I stepped on could cut, and what I used I could use up. Still, it was my time to go to this place to see where my body, mind, and spirit would meet and to see if what I had been imagining imagined me.

By the time Daniel returned, I was "sitting on *shpilkes*," a Yiddish phrase for becoming impatient. At breakfast, we said goodbye to Umberto, who wouldn't be flying with us. Any change felt unsettling as we were about to leave, especially separating from that sweet grandfather. Late, we hurried onto the van and drove away from Baños. We had a two-hour drive to the airstrip in front of us, a ride of a lifetime over and down the Andes on a dirt road to the oil town of Shell.

On the near side of the city, we passed a new hydroelectric plant. Its spray hit the windshield as we drove through a tunnel where the road turned into a ribbon. We were on the eastern slope of the Andes, in the rainforest, with primary jungle around us. Purple orchids waved on their stems as our van brushed by. The trees were thick and fruity, some bushy and others gigantically tall.

John pointed out scars on the far slopes, for which he felt a deep responsibility. Years ago, he had been part of a Peace Corps project that encouraged colonization to help Ecuadorians homestead in the rainforest. They cut out pieces of land for themselves so they could have a place to live and farm their crops. They cut into this irreplaceable arboretum, this herbal paradise, encroaching on the Indians and the natural habitat. With the canopy gone, the equatorial sun would reach the ground and bake it. The rains would wash more of it away. This meant diminishing food for insects and animals and taking away nests for birds. This meant, in some places, turning squares of the rainforest into dry fields, so cows could graze and eventually be sold for cash.

Seeing these scars, John spoke sadly but with a passion that, through awareness and action, included the possibility of reversal and of personal redemption. He now committed his life to doing what he could to save the rainforest, to authentically supporting indigenous people on their terms, to seeing life through the Indians' eyes, to transforming his own North American mind and actions, and to dreaming and helping others dream their lives in new, compatible, and sustaining ways.

We were along for more than the ride. None of us knew that John, a few years later, would reveal more of his pain and his guilty secrets in his memoir, *Confessions of an Economic Hit Man*. He would recount and account for the details of how he had convinced world leaders to carry more debt than their countries could afford, which brought recalcitrant regimes under the influence of the United States.

We drove through small communities, their strings of houses built close to the road. Streams of the Upano Amazon basin merged below and cascaded hundreds of feet to the biggest rivers in the east. Daniel, our new driver, slowed and swerved when he had to let a bus by. He talked to John more and more in Spanish the closer we got to Shell—a settlement the oil company had made as a jumping-off point for its jungle drilling.

By early afternoon, we reached the military checkpoint on the outskirts of town. At Miazal, we would be close to Ecuador's disputed border with Peru. Occasional fighting still occurred in that territory. The government wanted to know who was going in and who should be coming out. Daniel stopped the van in front of the striped wooden police gate. A young, armed sergeant took our passports and visas and showed them to an officer in the control booth. We were told they had to be held at the army base for safekeeping until we returned. "Never give up your passport," I remembered someone saying; however, relinquishing our papers was mandatory.

We ate in a small restaurant, more chicken soup and bottles of mineral water. The sick ate plates of rice. On a shelf in the corner, MTV rocked out its videos. An hour's plane ride from the Shuar, Madonna sang her version of "Truth or Dare."

I had flown in a small plane, a Cessna, once before. A friend of mine flew me over Lake Champlain, over our houses and the acres of apple orchards in our town. I felt safe in the vibration of that single engine and the light of those readable dials. For a few minutes, the pilot had let me fly, pulling the stick in and out, left and right. Flying the plane myself had made the story of my father's terrible Army Air Corps flight temporarily ease. In 1944, flying in Montana, taking his baseball team to another Army base for a game—my father was a physical education officer—the plane lurched. He was thrown against an exit door, which flew open. He was falling out. One of his players, the shortstop, grabbed him by his leg and pulled him back in.

I nearly lost my father before I was born. In the telling and retelling of that story, I inherited his fear of flying. When my grandfather died in California, my father didn't go to the funeral. He hadn't been able to fly again, to let go of old angers and his fear of the air.

On the runway, we weighed ourselves and our packs. Air Amazonas was a five-seat, thin-walled Cessna with twenty-eight thousand miles on its maintenance dial. Our teenage pilot, who looked like he'd had his first shave that morning, balanced our group by size. He didn't want us listing to one side or not lifting off. Flying with the first group, my shaky courage intact, I settled into the copilot's seat. The pilot gestured to me to buckle in and not to touch anything. "Don't worry, *señor*, I won't," I promised. I didn't need to test my wings. He revved the rubber-band engine and taxied onto the runway, a strip of broken road. Daniel and the others gave us the thumbs up as we bounced down the tarmac and eventually skyward, circling away from Shell and over the green carpet of jungle, over the muddy Amazon River. For a minute, a few roads stood out like veins. Yet soon we flew over green cover. John was sitting behind me, and when the canopy of the jungle came into view, he let out a yell of pleasure, an "Ah" of delight. He was going home.

We saw irregular brown squares where the forest had been cut for cows to graze. "Colonists," John moaned above the engine's drone. He understood what he saw. More than twenty percent, it is estimated, of primary Amazon jungle has been cut by farmers and burned by oilmen. Next to these spots, steel roofs reflected up at us. At a few thousand feet, I was still a passenger and an observer, going anywhere and flying in an idea and a dream.

As we flew through the cloud banks, the pilot talked, through static, to the dispatcher at his desk in Shell. I'd seen an old, crashed bomber next to the runway when we took off. I didn't see an opening in the canopy

we could use if our engine failed. Reading my mind, our young Sky King pointed over to the larger river, Rio Upano, to our right. *Our craft isn't a sea plane,* I worried to myself. Forty minutes later, we began to descend. *Where are we going?* I asked myself. *There's no place to land.* Suddenly, a green slice, no more than the length of a football field's mowed yards, appeared. We banked right and nosed straight in, wheeling over the trees, hitting the grass and mud like a tackled fullback. I tried to brake, jamming my feet on the plane's sheet-metal floor. We taxied to the strip's end where the trees started again. The pilot steered the plane around for his flight back.

I pushed open the small door, stepped onto the matted grass, and felt the wash of humid air. Bugs like black flies swarmed my bare ankles. *Here we go. Eat me up,* I thought. In fact, they were some of the few bites I would acquire in the jungle. I could have thrown my malaria pills away. Except for the one in Quito, I never saw or heard a mosquito and was told there were no cases of malaria in this area.

Together with the Indians who greeted us, Helmut, a six-foot-three Austrian, walked out of the grasses with his beautiful Shuar wife, Patrice. I thought he was Joseph Conrad's Kurtz. Yet he warmly extended his hand and grabbed our packs. With Don Juan, his seventy-year-old father-in-law, who was the Mission's leader and deacon, he and the Shuar had built the visitor's quarters we would stay in, down river, at Miazal. We walked a few  hundred yards to the river, Rio Mangosiza, behind the men—Mariano and his mute brother, Angel. Young and powerful, they spoke with their eyes. With a few swipes of their machetes, they cut branch seats to cross the gunwales of their hand-hewn canoes. We piled our packs between us. The Indians slung some of our gear on their backs. Quickly they poled into the river's slow current and steered us down that thread of the Amazon.

Flowers and bird songs spilled over the river's banks. The canoe rolled but didn't swamp. Gliding through the water, in the hands of those men, I felt my fear ebb away, stroke by stroke. Perhaps it was the happiness and relief of arriving, of letting go, and of exhaustion. Perhaps it was just being there. I didn't know what I would see and by what and whom I would be seen. I didn't know how to call what I saw by its real name. I lost myself in what I saw and heard, touched and smelled. In the middle of the earth's garden, I went to school again with the delight of a child. Overhanging vines swept the river banks. The forest crept to the edge of the water.

Later, Don said he saw an alligator slide under the water. I asked Daniel about monkeys. He said we were unlikely to see any. The Shuar hunted them, pushing them further into the jungle. The big anaconda lived in deep pools. One, we were told, swam out of the river onto a field and ate a calf. These were stories, someone else's facts. Here I was Mariano's guest, a guest of the forest.

After a half-hour of poling, we steered to a cut in the trees. The Shuar beached the canoes at Miazal, our base for the next two and a half days. We walked up a short bank, past two metal boats with outboard motors that Daniel used for going down river, and came to the lodges of Helmut and Don Juan and their families.

The compound was carefully laid out. A row of guest rooms lined one side of the square. An outdoor kitchen and roofed dining area stood across the way, with Helmut and Patrice's two-story apartment attached. Don Juan's house and a few buildings for tools and equipment were located nearby, along with pens for chickens and the ubiquitous guinea pigs. Fluorescent blue butterflies flitted among the trees and flowering red bushes. Helmut said if you peed on the ground, the butterflies would mass at the puddle and drink the salty spill. In the center of the small square, a hand-painted dove flew on a stone with the words *Paz en tu casa*—Peace in your house.

From the back of the building, I heard static talk from a two-way radio. John reported that Don Juan was speaking to the dispatcher at Shell. The weather was rapidly changing, and he was checking on the next flight carrying the rest of our group. As we carried our packs to our rooms, rain suddenly poured down and pounded the perfectly thatched roofs and turned the dirt to mud. This is why we needed rubber boots, and why we would emerge from the jungle covered in dirt.

Between groups of guest rooms, Helmut had built a traditional Shuar gathering room. A tall center pole supported the circular, thatched roof. A dozen hammocks were strung from the pole and attached to the outer walls like spokes from a hub. Benches were set around three of the side walls, and glassless windows looked out to the river and back to the square. A Shuar girl lit a kerosene lamp and provided punch and glasses for us. I felt welcomed and stretched out in a hammock. Rocking, drifting in my mind, I watched the sheets of rain. In this torrent, I was concerned that the others wouldn't be able to take off, or if they did, they would be caught in the weather. The rains slowed and stopped, and Don Juan came out of the radio room to say the plane was in the air and would land shortly. He greeted John with passion and all of us with love. "You said you would come back and you did," he said joyfully, embracing John. In his seventies, he had lived with the Shuar for more than twenty years as a pastor, healer, and friend. He'd married a Shuar woman and was father to three girls, Patrice, Maria, and Ester. Ester wasn't there; she had flown to Los Angeles to bring home her recently deceased husband. There was pain and anger in his eyes as he told us of the complications of retrieving the body and the obstruction of our government. He wanted nothing more than to bury his son-in-law at home.

Don Juan wore a beret, a scarf, a white, short-sleeved shirt, and white pants. He had arthritis in his neck and moved stiffly. The soreness didn't block his warmth. John told him our group was there to learn from the Shuar, to understand the problems they were facing, and to bring our cooperative efforts to bear in a way that would support the Mission's educational goals, the Shuar, and the survival of the rainforest. He smiled and went back to his radio.

Our rooms in the jungle were incredible. Each had two beds with firm straw mattresses, pillows, candles, glasses on a bed stand, and half-curtains that opened to a walkway edging the perimeter of our rooms. There was a bathroom with a sink, a cold shower, and a toilet, built by Richard, a Peace Corps volunteer who had installed a gravity-fed water system. How comfortable was I supposed to feel here?

As the rain stopped, I asked John if we could take a walk. Carolyn and Jane were interested, too. So we stored our things in our rooms and slid over the mud to the Mission at Miazal. We headed east, away from the square, on a wide, well-worn path, and passed a small house filled with t-shirts and other household goods. A young man standing inside with two boys greeted us in Spanish as we walked by. John remembered him from his last trip. "A young trader," he said. "Not Shuar. I'm not sure I trust him." We nodded back to the man. I wanted to poke my head in to see what he was selling.

We kept walking, past a field planted with scabby corn. "This is how the forest is cut to graze cows," John said. "It will never grow back to the way it was. This is why we must help them find local, meaningful solutions and stop cutting trees. We must take back what we see to help people in the North understand they must learn to need less and not be so greedy. But are we going to change ourselves first?" He spoke angrily, as he saw what was there and what was missing. "And we must be so careful not to tell the Shuar what to do. If they ask, we can share what we think, but it is we who must change our values, our behavior, and our needs!" It was impossible not to feel John's grief and his commitment. It was hard not to make his passion ours.

A few children strolled by us with their teachers. "*Buenas tardes*," the adults greeted us.

"*Buenas tardes*," the Indian kids giggled. It was about three-thirty. They were walking home at the end of their school day; we could have been anywhere in the world. Being with these children in Miazal, I thought of my son and daughter in Vermont. Yet quickly the nostalgia of that feeling shifted. Stepping to the left, around a bend, we came to a place I never imagined I would be facing. John, thank God, had not warned us about it.

A slatted wooden suspension bridge stretched ninety feet to the other side and sixty feet above the river. The bridge had no side rails. The floor-boards over the cables were less than four feet wide. Standing there, trembling, all I could see were scenes from *The Bridge Over the River Kwai*. But this wasn't a movie. If I wanted to get to the other side, I had to walk across the bridge and put one foot in front of the other. I thought of dropping to all fours, but I'm not sure that would have helped. Even terrified, I hadn't lost all of my pride. I didn't want the Shuar kids to have to walk over me.

Jane chanted and shook her hoof rattles. She said that for years she had been afraid of heights and more recently, this fear had turned into a debilitating phobia. She sometimes found it difficult to climb stairs. Anticipating this walk, she had done guided imagery and trance work to see herself less anxious in this situation. She asked me to give her plenty of room, stepped onto the bridge, and looked straight ahead. Weight on the boards, with the cables running underneath and along the sides, gave the bridge a swaying, bouncing stability. Like swimming in a strong wave, it was better if you went with the motion as it carried you forward.

Jane was halfway across when I stepped on. The sight of her walking, almost dancing from one side to the other, helped me look ahead. Close to the end, Jane let out a whoop that almost sent me over the side. I was almost there, too, and ready to scream in relief. The picture of my father, pulled back through the door of that Army Air Corps transport, flashed by. He had survived and so did I. On the bank, Jane wept happily. Each crossing of the bridge was liberating for her and confirming for me. Doing the next thing that needed to be done wasn't just one way, it was the *only* way.

Like a quarterback choosing his next play, John huddled the four of us together for a hug. A veteran, he hadn't forgotten what rookies go through. We continued walking, and around a small incline, past some blooming bushes, I saw the back of a building and a path to the Mission. We were at the school—Don Juan and Father Raoul's treasure. The buildings were set around the half-acre dirt square in symmetrical order. The boys' classrooms and dormitories on one side were mirrored by the girls' buildings on the opposite side. The village's church was next to the girls' lodge. We stood in front of the dining hall and a house used for offices next to it. In the square in front of the girls' craft house, a volleyball court was laid out. No, we weren't going to play there, having learned our volleyball lesson with the Quechuas in the High Andes. A full basketball court baked in the mud. The wooden backboards and netless, bent rims were nailed on hand-hewn poles. And yes, invited by the Shuar, we planned to play ball at noon the next day—hoops at the equator, in the jungle.

The square opened to the jungle at one end and back to the river at the other. In the middle of this area, with painted stones and wood, the Shuar placed a traditional design in the dirt. Tall totemic poles stood next to it. This was their space in which to be honored.

In the late afternoon, Mission life was quiet. I didn't know if the children were in their buildings or outside at some other activity. A teacher stopped to greet us on her way back to the bridge. Daniel told us the kids who lived here would do so for months at a time. To be a resident, a child had to live more than a two-hour walk from the Mission. The children who lived closer hiked back and forth each day school was in session along the narrow jungle trails before dawn, and again at dusk. "Even these kids," he said, "are afraid of snakes in the dark."

The Mission had been receiving a hundred and fifty dollars a month from the regional bishop, and that "donation" was about to be dramatically reduced to eighty—the money for food and school supplies would be almost cut in half. We weren't told the politics, yet being here only a few minutes, I felt sad and angry, the way I'd felt a few days earlier, standing at the shrine gilded in gold where the poor begged for alms at its doors.

We walked across the square to the trail. I wanted to walk further into the forest to see what was there. Away from the Mission, we passed a few Shuar lodges. They were the same as the ones we saw from the air as we flew to Miazal—thatched roofs, with branch sidewalls. Children looked over at us as we walked by. A few hundred yards from the square, we came to a larger building with boards stacked beside it. Inside, teenage boys hammered and sawed, crafting chairs and guitars. We walked closer and John said "hello" to the instructor, a reserved, wiry man who traveled from Cuenca every few months on a grant to teach the boys these skills. We asked if we could take pictures. "No, not of the Shuar boys," he said emphatically. I was moved by the strength of his statement.

Continuing on the path, John noticed how wide the trail was, uncharacteristic of the jungle, even though we were close to the school. It seemed as if we were on a road. John asked the teacher about it. He said the government was building a road through the jungle in order to reach the valuable salt deposits nearby. This road would connect to Macas, a town larger than Shell, located hundreds of miles away. It had been under construction for months and would be completed within the year.

We said goodbye and thanked him for allowing us to observe his class. John was filled with anger and sadness again. "Miazal will be changed forever," he said. "The roads come first, destroying the forest, and then the colonists." He saw the whole progression of loss that would push the Shuar further back into the jungle, cutting into their land and erasing more of their people and culture. Later, when John shared what we had been told, Daniel said he didn't think this was true. On and off, from different people, we heard conflicting versions of the government's intent and activities. John was unconvinced by these discrepancies. He had seen trees cut and promises broken. For some of the Shuar, perhaps the road meant jobs. For others it meant death.

We walked a little way further. The ground was muddy and saturated with rain. The next day we would hike with the young Indian men, those warriors who would wield their machetes and warn us about snakes, poisonous thorns, and plants. I didn't know what to look for, or what I was seeing in that damp beauty. My curiosity changed to caution.

At a crossroads of trails, we turned back to the Mission and stepped over a log that had a long string of leaves marching across it. The cutter ants carried their loads single file through time and against the chainsaw. John brightened as we passed a barely visible path into the forest on our left. "This is the way up to the Sacred Falls," he remembered. On his previous visit, he had hiked five hours with a friend and a twelve-year-old Shuar boy into the dense mountain, where they camped by the water. "The falls is the place of initiation for the Shuar, where boys become men, where they gain the spirit of the jaguar with their elders, and where they learn to use the power of *ayahuasca*, the visionary vine of the little death and their ancestors. Maybe we could hike there tomorrow." *Five hours further into the jungle*, I thought anxiously. *Spending the night among spirits and snakes?* Part of me wanted to see things in terms of what I knew and what I had already experienced.

A few months earlier, my son was bar mitzvahed, the rite of passage for Jewish boys. In mud season in Vermont, the weather is always iffy. That spring Saturday morning, we woke to the fields filling with a sleety snow—sugar snow or poor man's manure, the farmers call it. Almost the hardest task we had that day was slipping up our unplowed dirt road to reach the paved highway to drive to my son's ceremony.

I didn't know how I would manage to climb the muddy trail to the Sacred Falls, in the flowering, biting brush, in the scented darkness.

As we entered the square again, across the way, Peter, Stuart, and the rest of our group gathered. We embraced in a moment of reunion and of recognition. We were in the jungle, the rainforest, together—Indian and white, animal and plant, stone and spirit.

A boy stepped up on a stump behind us and reached for a large conch. Putting it to his lips, he blew it three times—like a *shofar*—in Hebrew, the ram's horn blown on Judaism's Yom Kippur, the Day of Atonement. It was time for dinner. The boys, who sat in front of their spear-decorated dormitory listening to a friend play his guitar, formed one line in front of the dining house. The girls stood in another line. They sheepishly looked at us. A few tried out their newly learned Spanish in greeting. Father Raoul, a grey-pony-tailed priest who had ministered to the Shuar for thirty years, joined them and waved to us. Daniel asked if we could see his house before we went back across the river. "Of course," he said.

It was getting dark. We walked across the square and down a path behind the boys' lodge. Father Raoul's round Shuar house stood on the edge of the forest. Chickens pecked around it. He had given each of them a woman's name, Daniel told us with a smile. In the morning we heard the priest call to his feathered sorority, this man who lived in simplicity and service, to whom the children came for blessing and friendship, and who had learned to heal with the power of a shaman.

We walked back though the shadows and recrossed the bridge in a line dance. Jane demonstrated her new courage and skill a second time, something we recounted as we swayed in our hammocks before dinner. The punch pitcher was filled and the three-log fire kindled. Its smoke coated the thatched roof for protection against chewing beetles. Daniel appeared with a fresh bottle of the high-proof trago whiskey. I sipped, awake in that warm dream, dozing in and out of our muted conversation. Helmut joined us and I heard pieces of his story. He had worked for the Congress of Racial Equality, lived in London, and now divided his time between Quito and Miazal. He had been in a relationship with a Swiss woman when he had first traveled to Miazal. Now he lived with Patrice. Helmut laughed like no one I've ever heard. He spoke directly, with passion and humor.

Around nine o'clock, we ate together—a banquet, cooked by Lucho, of pea soup, creamed chicken, bread, vegetables, and fruit. We toasted with Helmut's wine. We talked casually at first, then asked about the Shuar's practices of shrinking heads, of drinking *ayahuasca*, and of hiking to the Sacred Falls. Helmut didn't know of any head hunting in the last few years. Yet there was something in his voice that made me wonder. How would the government know what happened here? Had the Indian Federation—a coordinating body of tribal leaders—endorsed this change in practice? Someone asked him if he had ever taken the *ayahuasca*. "Yes," Helmut said cautiously. "It's very nice and very powerful."

I was still uncomfortable with the idea of taking this drug and drinking the distilled plant. I feared for my friends' sake, too. My grief of growing up with an addict flooded to the surface. What if someone freaked out? Died? What would my friends think of me if I didn't join them in the ceremony? How left out would I feel? How angry would my friends and their wives be with me if something terrible happened to one or two—or all of them? It was my invitation, and John's, that had brought them here. Fearful and taking on too much responsibility, I listened and ate.

Again I had the chance to transform each of these thoughts, to see them more clearly for what they were—attempts at controlling the future by replaying the past, and attempts at revising the past. I tried to create safety, or its illusion, mediated through fear and worry. However connected we were, each of us was responsible for his or her own decisions and *to* and *for* each other. This was another way to change fear, by trusting my intuitions and by knowing we were each capable of being in this world alone and together. I could revise—re-see—my way of being in the world by seeing these thoughts, attached to me like a wagon, for what they were and how they wanted to have a life of their own.

Cut the rope, I thought. *You won't die without your fear. If you ever need to, you can retie that knot.* I listened and took out my mind's knife, cutting through the strands of the rope. The strain of pulling a fearful self behind me let go. I felt myself break free. I let fear leave. I trembled into peace.

We decided to hike the next day up river along the Rio Tzurim, to the thermal waters—its own initiation, and not the same as the longer trek to the Shuar's Sacred Falls. Helmut had been there often. The last time he'd gone, he had walked with a group of Indian girls who had teased him about his size. "If you get hurt up there," they'd joked, "you're too heavy for us to carry home. We'll have to cut you up and bring you back in pieces."

Once, my family and I rafted down the white water of the Kennebec River in a fairly remote part of northern Maine. Our guides were licensed and told us a helicopter might be able to evacuate someone away from the river. If one of us were to break a leg or twist an ankle the next day in the jungle, how would we get back to the Mission? Each day taught me to prepare by not anticipating anything and to stand in front of the next door. Thinking, *what would I do if...*had become my way of life and part of my ability to imagine a future. I needed to trust my experience and to do what needed to be done.

I was exhausted with travel, conversation, and food. We said good night to each other and headed to our beds, lullabied by the river below, by the steady songs of crickets, by the black and orange frogs.

2

I SLEPT A HEAVY SLEEP OF SAND. I WOKE UP AND ASKED STUART IF HE WANTED TO GO for a swim before breakfast. No one had said anything about anacondas and piranhas in that part of the river. "Just swim with a friend," Daniel had encouraged, as if we were swimming in a town pool. We walked the short path to the water. The shore was sandy. The river flowed briskly. I waded in and ducked under, letting the current take me toward the middle. Stuart breast-stroked nearby and bathed at the same time. Over two thousand miles from the Atlantic, we swam in one of the rivers that eventually fed into the Amazon. I did think about snakes and killer fish, yet delight tempered terror; I left most of my fear with my boots on shore.

After twenty minutes, Stuart walked out of the river and toweled off on the bank. I swam toward him into the shallows. As I stood up I stubbed my toe against a rock and screamed, "Christ, my toe!" and saw its bloody flap. The skin swelled and my nail split. This was the same toe that had been spiked thirty years earlier in a high school football game—New Hampton School versus Kimball Union Academy. The nail had never healed and was one of those places on the body whose small wound is a continuing curiosity, a place to rub and ponder.

After all those travel miles and dangers, I had to stub my toe on the day we were hiking hours into the jungle? Or maybe the stone stubbed me, had been cursed and waited for my step. Prone to read meaning into everything—"You're making too much of this," my children often chided me—here the shamans said things often happened for a reason. Everything lived and dreamed its story forward. My toe throbbed and bled. I wondered what the river god was saying to me and what else she had in mind. I gently squeezed my foot into my rubber boot and adjusted my walk to its new limp.

We gathered for breakfast. Daniel said word had come back that at Martin's the next night, the shamans would have the *ayahuasca* prepared. He needed to know how many of us wanted to drink it. Five said "yes." I winced a bit as our group split into its necessary differences and individual preferences. Although I declined, surprisingly I imagined myself drinking, too. Whatever I experienced here allowed me to see myself in a new way, whether or not I actually did so. *Perhaps* and *maybe* moderated *never*.

As we walked back to our room, the young trader whose shop we had passed earlier that morning approached us and asked if we wanted to meet him and his friends—Angel, Mariano, and Jorge—at the Mission for a basketball game. Images of our joyful humiliation on the volleyball court in the High Andes with the Quechua crossed my mind. How could we resist the friendly invitation to redeem ourselves and to play what we thought of as "our" game? The women were getting their gear together for our hike. Daniel said, "Sure. Go ahead. There's time. We're in no hurry."

I worried about running and jumping with my bad foot in this "friendly" game. I couldn't wait to have the ball in my hands, as Boston Celtic Larry Bird had once said after scoring the winning basket against Michael Jordan in a playoff game. I squeezed my foot into the vice of my sneaker and followed the others back across the swaying suspension bridge toward the baked parquet floor of our Miazal Garden. As if we were in a neighborhood playground, we stood around the basket, taking shots—hooks and jumpers. Occasionally we roamed outside the invisible key to shoot an impossible three-pointer.

Men everywhere check each other out to see how skilled their opponents are, and to see what they're going to contend with. The Shuar, short and muscular, were quick as darts. They found the target of the wire hoop. Within minutes, we white globetrotters were sweating like pigs, and we were just shooting around as if we needed to "warm up." I motioned for us to form two lines for lay-ups, one for shooters and one for rebounders. Together, we turned that dirt court into a gym, and into the joy of a bunch of guys hanging out together.

We split ourselves into mixed teams, North and South Americans on the same sides—no *us* and *them* here. At first we played half-court and then, quickly, full court. The Shuar wanted to run and play a real game. In the jungle, heat was altitude. I looked over to Don, who was beginning to fry and fade in the equatorial noon sun. I didn't hustle to get back on defense. All thoughts of dominating with my size and experience disappeared in the water dripping down my body, in our shared playfulness, and in the true pleasure of new friends and teammates in the game. Fatigue overwhelmed me. In the second, abbreviated half, I shouted, "Next basket wins!"

On the run, Stuart translated this into his high school Spanish. Jorge, one of the two Shuar mutes, streaked toward the basket, traveling like crazy, and laid up the ball with a whoop for the winning score. Each team huddled and cheered the other, slapping high fives. The school kids who were crowded on the sidelines swarmed onto the court. They wanted the ball. They wanted to copy what they had seen us do.

We looked for the nearest shade, shared water, and took team pictures. The Indian men gestured to us to go for a swim with them. Gladly we walked to the river. On the bank, they stripped to their underwear. Most of them had a similar tattoo on their thighs—a mask-like design with characters that were half number, half letter. I asked Daniel about them. He

said they might have been soldiers in the army at one time and been inked when they were on duty.

We refreshed ourselves in that swim. The Shuar dove off a near rock and looked to us for a teammate's recognition. I had no idea that in the jungle I would feel as if I were back in Boston

as a kid, playing ball at the playground and not wanting to go home.

It was getting late. We had a hike in front of us. We gathered our things, hustled back across the bridge, and changed our clothes. We joined the others, who wanted to know who had won. Mariano, Angel, Jorge, and Lucho planned to hike with us. With Daniel leading, we waved *adios* to Helmut, Patrice, and Maria and walked again across our bridge of courage to the Mission and into the rainforest. We followed a black plastic pipe up to a concrete collecting box built by Richard, the last Peace Corps volunteer to serve here. It drew fresh water from the mountain river and fed it down to the village. I was pleased to hear how highly regarded Richard was, for some sense of national and humanitarian pride and for Peter and John, who had been volunteers, too. I wanted to see myself in their shoes, to imagine myself living among the Indians, learning by doing what I needed to know.

On the trail in the forest, we walked single file. We stepped carefully and watched where we put our hands. These paths were roads, turnpikes for the Shuar. They traveled for hours and days on them when they wanted to connect with other families and larger groups of people, when they hunted, and in previous days, when they went out in a head hunting, retribution war party.

We hiked sometimes in shadow, sometimes in light, depending on the thickness of the upper forest canopy. On the uneven terrain, I attended to each step due to my bruised toe and the slippery, protruding roots. Occasionally we climbed over or under a fallen tree and walked off the trail to avoid thickets that looked like they needed a chainsaw, not a machete. For the most part we stayed on the path. Sometimes we needed Daniel and Mariano to *thwack* an opening in the bush.

Twenty minutes out on one of those small detours, I heard a commotion behind me. I turned and saw Don and Peter running, hightailing it really, away from where they had been. At home, they were beekeepers and had been stung many times. This was different. We had heard of killer bees. Jorge held his right ear. His face twisted in pain. Because he was a mute, his screams were throaty grunts. He had been stung, and the venom was pumping into his head. Daniel dug into his red, waterproof pack and retrieved his sting kit. Like a surgeon, he placed a special syringe over the stinger and pulled out the plunger. Jorge howled. His tears streamed. He had just arrived from another part of Shuar territory, and these men had "taken him in" and befriended him. This was his first hike with his new brothers. He was embarrassed to show pain in front of us.

Daniel pulled on the needle a number of times, unsure of whether he had excised the killing thorn. Finally, the pain subsided. Jorge waved relief. Daniel, that moment's EMT, put away his instrument and pulled out a bottle of trago. He took a big swig and passed it to his patient, and then among us. I knew how dangerous walking in the jungle could be, but up to that point, that fact had been only a thought. I had denied the dangers I really didn't want to know and those for which I didn't have a name. It was necessary, life-saving, to be aware, to pay attention, and to listen to instructions.

We continued into the jungle, sobered by the stinging and warmed by the trago. From time to time, we forded Rio Tzurim to reach a more passable section of the trail. The current was fast, strong, and "pushy," a word a Maine guide had used to describe the Kennebec. We stretched ourselves across the river like beads, handing each hiker along a chain of others until we all reached the other side. At different points, Daniel, the naturalist, stopped to show us something we hadn't seen before—almost everything—and to explain the biology of the jungle. "See this little black and orange frog?" he said, kicking over a leaf with his boot. "It's poisonous. It could kill you. Here, black and orange means danger."

He particularly wanted us to understand the rainforest's ecology, why it was so necessary not to cut trees and not to let the equatorial sun bake the ground. Even with all the vegetation, the soil was very poor and thin. The root systems of trees, plants, and bushes primarily ran along the surface of the dirt. Decaying plant life produces a working bacteria—myce-lium—the jungle's necessary recycler of nutrients. "This process is nature's most necessary factory," Daniel said. "Without it, the forest is dying and is irreplaceable. Without it, we keep losing the bacteria, bugs, butterflies, and bananas we need to survive. We need it to be able to imagine and to see in our dreams. Biodiversity is a fancy word for ourselves, for all of life and its possibility for our future." I wanted to touch the mycelium, to rub it on my arms, and to eat it. Yet I needed to leave it alone and let it do its work.

In the first hour of hiking, the terrain was level enough for us to stop, for Daniel to name the trees and point out various orchids and red pas-sion flowers. He stopped to smoke a cigarette in a shallow, wide part of the river. My toe throbbed into numbness. I was afraid if I took off my boot, I wouldn't get it back on. I kept up with the group and thought it was better not to see what I couldn't heal. I didn't want to turn back alone or stay where I was. The river gouged the mountain it was coursing through. Ahead, the banks rose more steeply. The current was a rushing wind.

After another swig of trago, Daniel and the Shuar pointed us into the jungle. Our "walk" turned into an ascent. "Watch every step," Daniel warned, as we dug into the mud with our boots, stepped up to the next rock, and slipped on a stone or root. Again, we formed a chain. Each of us looked back to a hand that needed a hoist up and to an arm in front of us we could grasp. Small slips were okay. Anything big, and you could quickly tumble and crash down the embankment, seventy-five feet or more into the rocky river.

We weren't tied into each other by ropes or stepping on pitons. We climbed, determination linked through spirit. The Nike commercial flashed through my mind: *Just do it.* We put one foot in front of the other. We climbed alone and together, scratched and muddy, breathless and alive.

An hour into the climb, we stopped to catch our breath. Mariano pointed to a wider, deeper pool far below and said something to John. He gestured with his hands. John translated for us. This was where the giant anaconda lived—a boa so large it once rose from the river and swallowed a calf. This was the creature of which the Indians were most afraid. They never swam here. I thought of Scotland's Loch Ness monster and our own Champ, Vermont's fleshy, mythic version of the Creature from the Black

Lagoon submerged in Lake Champlain. An anaconda was another good reason not to slip, not to forget this wasn't my tenth hike in the jungle but my first.

Three hours into our two-hour walk to the thermal falls and to the Cascades Termica, we stopped for lunch—tuna sandwiches and soup, which Lucho found a way to cook where we were. The jungle scaled steeply around us, greener against the darkening sky. It rained lightly at first and then torrentially. Some of us huddled under a huge, overhanging rock. A few sat out in that thick shower, tired and soggy. Don "played" boa with Jorge. They dove, swam across the river, and surfaced delightfully near each other.

The rain pounded strongly. For the first time, Daniel looked concerned. The river could rise rapidly. He didn't know if we would be able to reach the falls, or if we would need to scramble to higher ground. The water edged higher on the rocks. How long could we be trapped here? Luckily, the rain thinned and the river stopped rising. Daniel said we still had a hard, shorter section to climb, and we needed to get going. He didn't want to run out of light at the end of the day.

It had taken everything for Nancy—brave Nancy—to come this far, and hearing what was left to do, she said, "I'm perfectly happy to stay here and wait for you to come back. I'll sit on this rock and look at the flowers and butterflies." She wasn't going any further. Daniel made sure she had enough water and sat in a safe place. We kept going with one less person, fearful of what could come out of the water for her and what could rise in her mind. We crossed the river once more and leaned into a steep embankment. Closer to the falls, I felt a surge of adrenaline, a "runner's high." The endorphins from anticipating the end of the hike kicked in. In the lead, Daniel stopped to throw some cans he found—someone else's trash—into his pack. John told us Daniel used three different trails to hike to the falls. He didn't want to overuse any one path or wear out anything forever.

At the crest of that ridge, we turned sharply down to the water. Word was passed back from the Shuar scouts, "Don't touch that leaf." Without room to maneuver, I danced under the branch's limbo pole. I wasn't going to brush that branch for the life of me.

Four hours from Miazal, the river narrowed into a mist. Mariano, Jorge, Lucho, Don, Stuart, Carolyn, and Macarena, the lead group, stripped down to their bathing suits and leaned blissfully against the mountain's rock, showered by the steaming falls spouting tens of feet onto their bodies. The rainforest encased us. Below the falls, the river pooled into a hot tub. We swam in the river of paradise.

Someone teased that he could see a resort's deck cantilevered over the river. "If a few rich developers reach here," Daniel said, "even that would be possible. We can't let that happen."

Next to the main falls, two others—one hot, one cold—tumbled into a pool. If we'd had a few more days together, we would have been naked and frolicking in that garden. None of the vines wore clothes! We swam forever in that hour until Daniel called us for the hike back to the Mission. Stuart motioned for me to look back at the ledge next to the falls. Jorge was standing at attention. He grinned widely and saluted us, the river, and his new Shuar comrades.

The afternoon was ending. It had begun to get dark each night by six-thirty. We needed to start back. The best way down was *in* the river. Where it was too fast or deep, we exited the water and climbed around. We walked, stumbled, and floated down the river. Without that morning's goal of reaching the falls, I did feel more anxious. I thought about the present dangers—being swept away, breaking a bone, or twisting an ankle. I worried about being rescued. I listed the skills I didn't have. I flooded myself with fear, countered by one thought: I wanted to get back to Miazal and stay safe for my wife and children. Too much thinking was disastrous. I needed to keep focused, put one foot in front of the other, reach back to pull someone forward, and reach ahead to be pulled down the river bed.

Macarena and a few others had fallen behind. They said she had lost one of her rubber boots, a necessity on those rocks and terrain. Don and Jorge walked back and dove for it. Peter and Stuart stationed themselves down river to spot it in the fast current. We all looked for her boot camouflaged in the water. Gracious and determined, Macarena wanted us to move on. She said she would be all right. Finally, that was what we had to do. With an extra sock for another layer of protection, she swam and walked with us with strain on her face and determination in her eyes.

A third of the way down, we reached Nancy. What must it have been like for her, sitting alone on a boulder in the river, surrounded by the jungle? She spent her hours watching the brilliant blue butterflies flit above the water. She counted the varieties of flowers. She was perfectly content. She looked serene. Nancy was courageous and comfortable being alone with herself.

Hand to hand, we climbed up, down, and around the slippery, rocky banks and cliffs. It was no use thinking what could happen. As Don said later, we walked in white light—a light we made. We let it touch us and change our fear into action. We were tied in and together by the incredible human instinct and will to live, to thrive through connection and shared purpose. We were tempered by what we could lose and by the knowledge that we could die in the river, in that living and dying forest. We came to one last fording where the river, filled with rain, rushed in a frenzy. The Shuar men stood on critical stones. We handed each person through the fierce current. On the other side, I was too tired to scream with relief and pride. I walked the last mile to the Mission without saying anything.

The path took us by trees whose palm leaves could be used to make hats—Panamas. We walked through scrubby corn fields where the forest had been cut and cows grazed. Finally we arrived at the school buildings we had left earlier that day. The bridge felt as steady as a road after that hike.

Back in our room, I looked at myself in the mirror. My blue ban-dana was rolled into a rope, tight around my forehead. My Otter Creek Outfitters t-shirt was muddy and drenched. I had promised to wear it in the jungle for Jerry, the store's owner, who had graciously lent me his own pack. My nylon running pants were shredded and ripped from stretching between rocks. I stripped them off and threw them away. I had almost forgotten about my right toe, which by then was numb in the tourniquet of my boot.

Sitting on my bed, holding my foot out, I needed Stuart to pull off my boot. My toe swelled in that release. It had been cut by my nail, and the flesh blossomed into a deep bruise. We had another hike the next day to the shaman's lodge, and eventually to the airstrip and our link to home. I limped to the shower. Blood drained into my toe. I had released a back spasm earlier that day by bringing to mind the healing work of my friend Beata, a therapeutic masseuse, so I thought I could reduce the swelling in my toe, "icing" it by thinking the word "subside." After my shower, I gingerly put on my sneaker and hobbled to a hammock in the community room. This was an injury that would take more than thoughts to heal.

By then, it was fairly dark. The round, open room was lit with kerosene lamps and a glow from the ever-burning, three-log fire. I slipped into the hammock and relaxed in its swaying. I exhaled a breath I had been holding for hours, perhaps for years. In hiking and swimming, slipping and stumbling, and climbing up and down, part of me had died or had been changed. I had transformed a fear larger than my body—the fear of being afraid. I breathed new air, a breath I felt fully inside me. I inhaled the world.

In that moment, I remembered that I was born with my umbilical cord wrapped around my throat—a blue baby. Rocking in the fatigue and for-tune of Miazal, I felt that cord unravel and fall away. I took a full breath. A stone had been rolled away from the door of my mouth. I wasn't asleep. I wasn't awake. I drifted in the trance of the smoke and the shadowy, shifting light. I was the same and different, old and new.

We talked quietly. Carolyn sat down on the other end of my hammock for a few minutes before she joined Jane in hers. In the smoke, I didn't know who was talking with whom. Something changed among us in that climb. We had ventured out and returned, alone and held by each other. If I drank more than a sip of trago and fruit punch, I would fall asleep. Even a little of that fire water was enough to smooth my muscle soreness and calm my swollen toe.

We walked across the square to the dinner table and Lucho's soup, chicken, rice, vegetables, and fruit. Helmut poured wine for us. As we ate, we talked. The conversation seemed tentative at first, as if we didn't know how to say what we were feeling or what we had experienced together. Perhaps we were anticipating the next day's hike in the jungle to Martin's lodge and the shaman's *ayahuasca*.

Then the conversation moved sharply to what was in our consciousness, on the edge of our exchange with ourselves and our Ecuadorian friends. What was the crisis for the rainforest and its people? In what ways were we Westerners and Northerners responsible for its damage? How could we take appropriate responsibility and change our attitudes and actions? How could we listen to what was requested and required of us, to work with indigenous people as they defined and voiced their own needs? How could we protect the rainforest and save ourselves, too—what we felt as the soul of the earth in these trees and flowers, people and rivers?

Spiritually and practically, we sought solutions and a process to solve the "problem." We wondered what could stop the destruction, knowing that an imposed solution is unwanted and uninvited and that the "fix" can sometimes keep things as they are and addict the patient to the cure. If the Shuar needed money—hard currency—to buy necessities, including the land that was already theirs, what could they sell that wouldn't require cutting and burning the rainforest? Could they sell plants and crafts for export? Could they raise bees and ship honey? Could they be paid not to cut trees? What would be desirable and culturally meaningful for them in a world that encroached on them, a world they had been forced to encounter—the world of multinational oil companies?

Helmut sat at one end of the table and Daniel at the other. Patrice and her sister, Maria, worked and listened in the kitchen. I sensed the tension between our wish to translate goodwill into active commitment and what they must feel when there was an urge to fix—people doing something for, or to, others without their acknowledgment or consent. Was our talk, however innocent and well-intentioned, a violation?

Daniel stood and walked away from the table, away from the candle-light and into the darkness. Had we offended him? Were we repeating the problem he had been teaching us about? When he returned, Helmut tried to engage an idea Peter had suggested based on his knowledge that US farmers were paid, at times, not to raise certain crops. Here, this idea would mean actually counting trees, paying Shuar families not to cut them down, finding a way to administer and record this project and make it meaningful to the Shuar on their terms.

This proposal irritated Daniel. Helmut wanted to keep exploring the idea. He wished to consider any new thinking, any workable practice that could be suggested—a format that has been engaged (not without contro-versy) by other countries. Unknowingly, we had walked into an old argu-ment between these two—a spider's web.

Helmut asked Patrice and Maria to join us. He wanted them to say what they thought. Patrice politely laughed at the idea that the Shuar could be paid not to cut trees. Maria agreed. Helmut wanted Daniel to hear that it wasn't necessarily the particular concept that was important, but that a new notion was suggested and put into the conversation by a person of integrity. He knew the well-intended can be misinformed, even harmful. Was the degree of disagreement a result of a deeper cultural misunder-standing, as well as language differences among us?

The next day we learned something that weighed more immediately on Daniel, and that was part of his pain and frustration that night. Passion engendered passion, and with his sister-in-law, Maria, sitting with us, Helmut, warmed by the wine, asked if he could share something that deeply angered him. At the risk of embarrassing Maria, he told us she had been invited to Texas to visit a family she had met in Miazal. In two trips to the American Embassy, she had been turned down for a routine visa, and she and he had been treated disrespectfully. Helmut had worked for the Congress on Racial Equality and knew racism when it faced him.

I felt angry, sad, and embarrassed, feelings shared by my friends. In a few days we would return to Quito. We said we would go to the Embassy to protest this decision and that treatment. Maria felt disappointment and outrage, too. She was reluctant to support our response. She didn't want to have her hopes raised again and to incur more humiliation. Helmut supported our reaction and plan. He let us know what he thought and felt.

This event was framed, too, by the difficulty Don Juan and his youngest daughter, Ester, had experienced when claiming the body of her husband, who had died in Los Angeles and finally was on his way home. Even with these insults—the killing of trees, land, people, and trust—Helmut, his family, and Daniel extended their welcome, and they invited us to join their dreams.

We ended the evening teasing each other about who wouldn't be able to eat Lucho's special breakfast the next morning because they were required to fast in preparation for drinking *ayahuasca*. Helmut walked us back to our rooms carrying his fluorescent flashlight. He trained the beam on the trunk of a tree. Blue, yellow, and green beetles shined back at us, flashing their neon signs.

3

STUART WANTED TO WALK BACK TO THE MISSION SCHOOL ONE LAST TIME. HE wanted to leave the t-shirts he had brought with the children. He wanted to take a few more pictures to share with his students at Deerfield Academy in Massachusetts. As we walked by the classrooms, the students looked out at us, poking one another and smiling. Two teenage Shuar boys ran by, late for class. I tossed an orange I had saved to one of them. It took him by surprise. He caught it and flipped it to his friend for inspection before they ducked through the classroom door.

Peter and Don walked toward us from the far end of the square. They had gotten up early and hiked into the jungle looking for the next settlement, another cluster of Shuar houses. "*Buenos dias*," we greeted each other in passing, like old residents. Even as friends, I felt a reserve among us as we prepared to hike to the shaman's lodge and leave the Mission. In a few days, we would be saying goodbye to Ecuador, too.

As we walked to breakfast back at our compound, someone said Daniel was ill and was going to stay in bed until it was time for us to leave. Daniel, our guide and godfather, our doctor and pharmacist—sick? Lucho prepared a tasty meal of fried banana crepes and warm rolls served with guava jam. Anyone taking *ayahuasca* was warned not to eat and to keep an empty stomach. The hallucinogenic plant caused vomiting and diarrhea in the first minutes after ingestion. Maybe that's when I made my final decision not to drink. The crepes smelled too good. I've never been one to turn down a sweet plate of anything.

Truthfully, it was more that the soulful reasons for which I had come to Ecuador and to the jungle had been fulfilled on our climb to the thermal falls. I felt complete, having risked losing myself in fear, risked the possibility of accidentally dying surrounded by vanishing people and plants. Beyond my limited past experience with pot and with the history of addiction in my family, I knew I didn't need to drink this "vine of the soul." I didn't need to change the way I was feeling or what I was seeing. There was enough in what I had already experienced to keep me open, and to keep opening me. I hoped this wasn't a decision made from anxiety or false superiority. I felt clear within myself, fully in my body and spirit. I had concern for my friends. They were making their own decisions. We would be together.

I made my way back to our room and gathered my things. We would spend the night in Martin's lodge and not return to the Mission, so we needed to take only what we could carry. The Shuar would bring what we left behind to the airstrip the next day. I wound up with everything I brought on my back. John was right. I didn't need the stack of books I had with me. There was enough to read in what I saw.

By Helmut's apartment, Macarena and Jane stood next to Patrice. She brought out some ceremonial shells and nut belts to sell. I imagined my son and daughter adorned in them. Buying a few things was part of the ritual of saying goodbye, of wanting to take something I could hold with me, and of wishing to blur the line between resident and guest, friend and tourist. Patrice handed me a bracelet made of iguana skin—a band from its body—a gift of friendship. It was too small for my wrist, so she and Maria took me to the outdoor washing faucet to soap my arm. I felt honored by their persistence. They stretched the hide so it would fit, so I could wear it home. Dried, the iguana skin would curl and tighten around my wrist. Wet, it would loosen and slide like a snake.

Daniel appeared. His illness was only a rumor. He said he had been in the radio room talking with Don Juan, who wanted to meet with us before we left. We piled our packs together and gathered in the smoky community room. Don Juan and Daniel joined us. We talked and listened to what we needed to hear and be told.

With John sitting next to him to translate, Don Juan looked around our circle. He wanted to know who we were and what work we did. John explained that we were committed to finding ways we, individually and as a new group of friends, could respectfully support the Shuar, the Mission, and the rainforest, and that we had discussed these concerns at dinner. Through this experience we were finding ways to see ourselves differently, and to find things in our own thoughts and actions that needed to be recognized, understood, and changed.

Don Juan nodded. He told us how pleased he was with our interest and with the feeling he sensed among us. He was gratified that we had come. Without making any request of us, he told us the regional bishop had cut the Mission's allocation for funds in half, and this would seriously affect the education and support of the Shuar children. He had learned how to survive, to do his work on very little money over the last twenty years, and he would again. He thanked us for our presence and said he hoped we would return. Standing, he shook hands with each of us. He had to leave to prepare for the return of his son-in-law's body—Don Juan the deacon, Don Juan the healer.

Daniel thanked us, too, for our desire to translate our experience into some useful and necessary action. It was extremely important to him that we be agents of change; he brought only a small number of people here. He wanted to know more about our ideas and seemed to hear the range of possibilities differently than he had the previous night. He had talked with Don Juan; perhaps that counsel, and a new day, had tempered his skepticism.

Daniel had been coming to Miazal for nine years. With tears in his eyes, he said the support of these children was one of his life's missions. The Shuar's respect and love for him were palpable. His picture hung above the dining table, together with those of Don Juan and José, the principal of the school. It had taken a long time for the Shuar to trust him. Even though he was a Jew, he had participated in a number of Christmas celebrations at the Mission. He told us the spirit here at that time was incredible. At the turning of the year, it was here he most wanted to be. "I hope you'll find a way to keep your connection to us," he said. Sitting in that lodge—classroom and shrine—I was in the heart of Ecuador, one of the hearts of the world.

Daniel left us to ourselves so he could get his things ready for the two-hour hike to Martin's house. We sat in silence, held in that blessing and that challenge. What did we want to do? What could and should we do? These questions were no less than asking what was the purpose of life—my life. What was I going to do with these people, this place, and the life that connected us? If every moment is an accumulation and a readiness for the next moment, how was I going to take this experience into my next breath and my next step? The words of Joseph Campbell came to mind. How was I going to take these events and turn them into experience? I hadn't expected how clearly the questions would present themselves and how quickly my life would compose itself into one of its necessary answers.

I left that meeting as I do a funeral or a graduation. Something had been buried, the earth dug out and turned over, prepared for a new planting. Together in the square, we were loaded with gear, goodbyes, and a lifetime of thoughts and feelings. We stepped away from the Mission without walking away. For ten minutes we walked a wider trail, with Rio Mangosiza to our right and rainforest and scrubby pasture to our left. Quickly that trail turned into a path, a humid, viny corridor in the jungle. The idea of a "walk" compared to a "climb" was appealing, but carrying a backpack in the jungle at midday at three thousand feet was strenuous, too. The tree roots were slippery. The mud on small embankments almost took me down. We hiked in single file, slowly enough to talk. Daniel said it was important that no one wander off alone. On the path, walking in a group, with the Shuar in front of us and behind us, we were protected. Alone, we could be prey to our own curiosity, to stingers, and perhaps to the invisible darts of enemy shamans.

A half-hour from the Mission, we passed a Shuar mother and her daughter heading toward Miazal. She greeted us with a nod. *What does she think,* I wondered, *coming across this string of gringos and Indians on the* trail? We were each going where we needed to go.

I sweated like crazy. Thirsty, I worried about how much water we'd brought with us. A few days earlier, Daniel had teased us. "You guys drink enough water to swim in. You change your clothes so often, you'd think you were going out dancing," he'd quipped. *It's true,* I thought. *When you have a constant supply of water, like we do in the North, it's nothing to keep filling a pitcher of water or to put another load of wash in the machine.*

John and Maria walked behind me. She was a trained nurse. I felt reassured that she was with us, as a Shuar and as a professional. Although I increasingly trusted our shared ability to respond to whatever we incurred, whatever would face us, I was glad she would be with us at Martin's for the *ayahuasca* ceremony.

After a few hours, we came to a small opening in the jungle by a river. "This is a good place to stop and rest, before we finish our hike," Daniel said, taking off his pack. I sat on a rock and soaked my bandana. Maybe this walk would be twice the distance we'd thought it was going to be, like the previous day's hike. Finally, our days of travel, of taking everything new in and to heart, had taken its toll. I was tired, hot, and crabby. Overall I felt little, if any, anger or irritation during those days. Our group's sensitivity, caring, and accommodation was a salve for what a farmer neighbor of mine calls "any case of the nerves."

We regrouped and stepped across the narrow river. John pointed out a basket-like trap in a dammed-up section of the water. "The Shuar put the plant 'barbaso' in this pool," he said. "It takes the oxygen out of the water. The fish die here and are caught in that weir." A few fish were snagged in their homemade mesh. Perhaps a fisherman was close by and watched us as we sloshed across the stones.

Back in the jungle, the path turned very muddy. I stepped forward and jerked my foot out of the sucking dirt. Carolyn was in front of me and knee-deep in a small swamp. She was distressed. How quick and alive was that sand? The others were not in sight. I climbed onto a log that had fallen across the muck and reached down to her, so she could use my arm as a rope. Carolyn pulled herself up. Months later, she wrote me that her worst fear was being sucked down in quicksand. She met her terror there as if it was waiting for her, inviting survival and transformation. I had no idea what this meant to Carolyn at the time, yet I was glad to reach out to help her move through, as a way of taking another step myself. She and I walked together for a while, and perhaps in anticipation of that night's ritual, we shared that we had both grown up in alcoholic families. We were, each in our own way, recovering persons.

Jargon aside, I have always liked the word "recovering," not so much in the sense of "getting over something," but because there is something in our lives that it is necessary to recover and retrieve. This is especially true when, as children, we have been affected by someone else's alcoholism and then get caught in our own addictive attempts at quieting our anxiety and grief. Carolyn and I were both familiar with recovery language in the letters ACOA—adult child of an alcoholic—and with the healing ritual of twelve-step meetings. I felt calmer in the shorthand of that knowledge. We didn't know each other well, yet there was a common thread to this aspect of our lives—what it meant to be walking into a night, however "different this time," where we would be in the presence of people drinking *chicha*— Shuar beer—and using an hallucinogenic drug.

It's hard to explain this experience to someone who hasn't grown up with that kind of turmoil and unpredictability, even when we each have our own family wounds. It's hard to say how automatic one's responses become in order to survive being raised by a chemically impaired parent—how you fruitlessly try to control, manipulate, cure, and distract the addict's drinking. I tried to be the best and the brightest, not knowing I was trying to cover my fury and sadness with the temporary balm of personal achievement. Confronting fear on this journey, I brought back the ghost of this childhood grief. I needed to say goodbye again to my mother's bottles—those fifths. I needed to say goodbye to my father's anxious phone calls and to the impact of addiction on my sister and me that I carried in my heart. I needed to see the next step in front of me and take it.

Almost in unison, Carolyn and I turned to each other and said, "If anyone gets drunk or trips out of their mind, I'm not responsible for taking care of them." This was another way of continuing to heal our days of trying to save a parent. Rejoining the others, I knew I had Carolyn as an ally. In the night we walked toward, we could sit together in the steps of a new way of being and our own healing ceremony.

Ahead, off the trail, a dog barked. *This must be Martin's*, I thought. We kept walking and came to the edge of a corn field. I stepped into that field of dreams like Ty Cobb in the movie of that name, not knowing where I would emerge on the other side. By this time, three hours from Miazal and even with the terrain relatively flat, my t-shirt was soaked in the day's humidity.

As we walked single file, military-like, I thought of my friend John Coffin, who lives in South Hero, Vermont, and who had been hit by a bullet during the "undeclared" war in Thailand in 1969. Stuart, another of my veteran friends, walked in front of me. He had written me a letter from Long Bihn Base the night he had pulled perimeter duty and gotten shelled by Viet Cong mortars. I remembered my college lacrosse teammate, Bayard Russ (a great goalie, whose nickname was Bye-Bye), who said, "I want to be where the action is," and who, as a Marine, couldn't stop the bullet that killed him. I imagined my next-door neighbor, Dwight Dunning, who built bridges during the war. I thought, too, of Patrick Stine, the army's last ENT physician to leave Saigon. I saw myself again at Fort Sam Houston in Texas—not shot, walking safely and guilt-ridden past the burned soldiers evacuated from Southeast Asia for treatment.

How could those men, hiking in the jungle, sweating like pigs, carry themselves and their rifles, ammunition, radios, and everything else they needed for a day's fight? How could they fire back in the heat, amidst the turmoil, among those leaves and vines? What would I have done in their place? Would I have come home?

A week before I left for Ecuador, Coffin and I met for lunch in Vergennes, Vermont, billed as the smallest city in the world. John walked in with a warrior's stick he had been given by his martial arts master. A few heads turned when this former offensive tackle set down his stave, fit for Robin Hood's Little John. We rekindled our old friendship. We found we had many new things in common. We wouldn't have to rely on the past in order to carry on a conversation and enjoy each other's company.

We talked about what we thought it meant to be a man, and to be masculine. What did we each think about the "men's movement," which was being portrayed by the glossy press as men going off on weekends to chant and drum? As former football players, did either of us still want to block, tackle, and hit someone? John told me he had recently almost been in a fight with a guy he knew, in a parking lot after his Tai Kwon Do class. They'd argued, he said, over something stupid.

If a man wanted to test himself and to show "courage," how could he do it? What was the difference between macho and masculine? I loved that we were beginning to know each other again, outside of a dormitory, and not in the routine of a fall football practice but through our wandering talk—two men watching what they were eating with a spear lying beneath their table.

I told John about my fears as I was about to leave. "No shit," he quipped. And without blinking, he looked straight into my eyes and said, "If you die there, I'll tell your children you were a man of courage." I felt like weeping when I heard those words from my freshman year co-captain, a soldier who had been in combat.

Not surprisingly, I remembered a stone I had thrown in sixth grade that had slashed my friend's forehead. I could pick it up with his blood on it. I couldn't take back what I did. I could fight with him if I had to. I could go home and tell my father everything or nothing. I could walk away. I could go to the jungle. In that noontime conversation, I was in John's platoon. He had written a letter home to my parents about my courage, and I needed to read it. We paid the check and, standing there, grabbed each other—something between a hug and an embrace.

Back in the jungle, our line bunched up, standing on one end of a huge log whose upper surface had been scraped out with a machete. Daniel hooted loudly toward the hill in front of us. We were near the lodge where the shaman, Charapa, Martin's father-in-law, lived. It was customary for friends to announce and to warn of their approach. We walked by Charapa's dwelling and through his vegetable fields. "He grows everything he needs here," Daniel said, naming the crops, which included cotton. "He and Martin hunt meat for their families in the jungle." We slid down one more dip and climbed to a place from which we could see the river, the same water that, miles back, flowed by Miazal. A few hundred yards further we came to Martin's lodge, our last stop in the rainforest.

Martin's house, long and oval, was built in a small clearing. The thickly thatched roof was supported by walls of sticks bound closely together. A scattering of hens and ducks and a rooster clucked, quacked, and crowed around the house. A few ran in and out of the front door and picked the dirt floor clean of insects. Two girls peeked at us from the far end of the building. A heavy smoke hung in the air.

Martin came out to greet Daniel and motioned us through the front entrance, a narrow stick door tied on a vine hinge. Daniel told us to sit quietly around the perimeter of the front room and not to go behind, where Martin and Charapa sat, and not to venture into their sleeping and cooking space. Custom was everything here—order in space, time, and conversation. I ducked my head and followed the others in.

It was dark and smoky. Light streaked through slits in the branch walls. Twenty-five feet away, Charapa sat in front of one of the two fires in the house. Martin and his wife, Luisa, sat to his left. Martin chatted with Daniel and they exchanged news of their families. This was the way Shuar greeted each other when visiting—talking and laughing in low voices. I perched on a log. My back began to ache as if I had been sitting in meditation. I was too nervous to stretch, so I looked around at each of us, breathing in and out the reality of where we were—guests in that lodge for the night, participants in ceremony, and in the realm of *ayahuasca*.

Martin and Daniel ended their greeting. Luisa dipped her gourd bowl into the large iron pot in front of her that was filled with *chicha*, the home-made beer the women had brewed. She fingered off the foam on the rim and served her husband, her father, and her dear friend Daniel first, and then came to each of us in the circle three times. I sipped the lumpy, yeasty beer, which was warm, sweet, and refreshing. The stock of the beer was made from the manioc plant, which was first chewed by the elder women until it was ready for brewing. Anthropologist Michael Harner, friend of the Shuar, has reported that Shuar men can drink large amounts, even gallons, of *chicha* a day. We drank what the women had made in their mouths.

After drinking, Daniel looked to us, indicating that we had passed through the first phase of our visit. We could relax, unpack, and hang our things by our sleeping bags. Within the hour, we would walk to the river to swim and bathe before returning for dinner—those of us who could eat—and the evening's ceremony of singing, seeing, and seeing the songs. Daniel again warned us that we should not go off by ourselves. Stepping outside and behind the lodge, I saw into the kitchen. Children and women sat and prepared food. I recognized the traditional Shuar fire—three logs pointed into a center flame. Was that a man asleep on a raised mat bench?

We walked a short, muddy path. Daniel pointed out two different spots we should use if we needed to pee or shit. Each was placed to keep run-off from contaminating the living quarters. We went through planted corn and came to a cleared square, not unlike the Mission's. A soccer goal and volleyball net stood at one end, and at the other, a lodge like Martin's house, recently built for local gatherings. It was late afternoon. Our shadows stretched across the dry dirt field and court.

On the far side, we stopped by a patch of manioc and stood by Luisa, who cut the low plant with a few chops of her machete. Her elderly mother stood barefoot beside her and sang her song of thanksgiving to the earth for giving its fruitful blessing. We watched, yet this wasn't a show. Her words, melody, and voice wove into her cutting. She sang as she dug a hole with a long stick next to the harvested plant and then planted a new root that would grow into another manioc and another song.

Martin smiled when we asked if we could take his family's picture, a smile of tolerance and pride. They stood in the bronze light as if they were at a county fair. Martin, Luisa, and their three young children looked beyond our cameras and out to the world.

Grateful for the chance to swim, we walked a short path to the river's banks. They were steep and muddy. The water moved swiftly. I stripped to my bathing suit and followed Don and Martin. Trying to break my slide, I grabbed the nearest tree and felt the sting of a thorn pierce the fleshy pad of my left thumb. I winced and thought of the story that José Pineda, the shaman in Otavalo, had told Jane about her back pain—that once she had stepped on a thorn that held the dust of death on it even though it wasn't meant for her. I checked to make sure the needle wasn't in my hand, and like Teta Marcos, the *curandero* who had cleansed and rebalanced me, I sucked the blood from the wound and spit it out. I tried to break any curse that may have been meant for me or anyone else.

I reached the river and tiptoed on some stones to where the water was deep enough to dive into. I dove under and felt the fast current pull me into its underwater path. Surfacing, I stroked to get closer to the shore and into the quieter water. Don and Martin, in Olympic form, swam upstream and across the current to a sandbar. They stayed there while we swam, talking to each other with their voices and their hands. Above us, Charapa, the shaman, squatted and watched over us. For the first time in our days in Ecuador and in the jungle, the insects began viciously biting. John's body swelled with welts. Frantic, we stepped out of the water, dressed, and climbed the bank to head back to the house. Light shaded into twilight.

At Martin's, Lucho prepared pea soup for those who could eat because they weren't going to drink the *ayahuasca*. Behind the center dividing wall, the women talked quietly and prepared the meal. Guinea pigs squeaked in their pens. A child lit candles throughout the lodge, lending it a sense of Sabbath or Mass. Daniel told us it was appropriate for us to walk, in pairs, back into the kitchen and family sleeping area. The women sat closely together and tended the simmering meal. The youngest children squatted around their mothers and aunts. They were stirred into the broth of conversation. No Shuar raised her voice. Rarely did a child cry. What was in their culture that muted their expression and amplified ours? Surely I couldn't read the subtle messages they were signaling to each other with their hands and eyes.

As we sat by the half-open door, a thin, older man walked in. He carried something under his arm I couldn't make out. The Shuar men greeted him. He had brought his own bowl for *chicha*. He sat down a few feet from me and looked with interest around our gathering. I said, "*Hola*," anx-

iously. He nodded back. I wished I could speak with him, and sat in a frus-
trating silence. Someone whispered to me that he was Chumpi, Charapa's
friend, another shaman and musician. He carried a two-string violin, and
he would help lead the ceremony and the healing. The two men talked and
laughed, *kibitzing* like clubhouse card players.

I don't know what I expected for the beginning of the healing and for
the visioning. Very quietly, those drinking the *ayahuasca* were asked to sit
by the shaman, who painted three thin, reddish lines across their cheeks
and noses. I felt excited and apprehensive, as each of my friends was painted and as each put on what athletes call a "game face." Having chosen not
to drink yet wanting to be included, like a kindergartner, I asked Daniel
if I could have my face painted, too. "Painting is only for those drinking,"

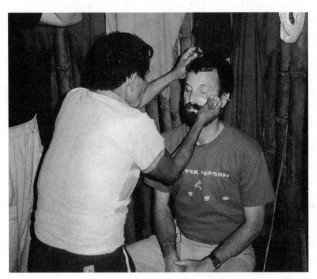

he said. I should have
known I wasn't going
to get something for
nothing. It was good
to have the integrity of
the ritual confirmed.
Truthfully, I was con-
tent with my decision
to be here, in a way
I mistakenly thought
was only to watch and
listen.

Daniel motioned to
them to come forward
one at a time for the
natema—the vine of the soul. The two shamans ladled a shot-glass's worth
of the thick, hallucinogenic syrup, which had been brewed and distilled
over eight hours, into a cup from which the five people drank. Some of the
children gathered around us, clearly familiar with this custom. Without
fanfare, the ceremony began. Like everything else here, it was woven natu-
rally into the moment, the next breath, and the next step.

I sat on one of the raised mat beds. A shaman entered the door and
danced down the center of the lodge. He wore a mask and shook his

rattles. That image has stayed with me, somewhere between memory and dream, in what the Shuar call the real supernatural world. I don't know if this happened. It is the image to which I return whenever I imagine myself back in Martin's house. I see what occurred and what I think occurred as its own combined and complementary reality.

The participants found seats around the room on logs or on one of the three raised palm leaf beds. They waited for *Arutum,* the spirit of power and knowledge—the vision—to come to them. Told to sit quietly and concentrate, they anticipated a wave of nausea to take them outside the house into the brilliant moonlight, so they could vomit. This would announce the presence of spirit and that visioning was possible. Because they had fasted, they were temporarily sick. Then they could use the intensity of sensory experience. They could see things and themselves as they are and see the jungle's natural apparitions. They could meditate on questions meaningful to their lives. They could see inside things to what was there to be seen.

I sat next to Carolyn, safe in the connection we had made earlier that afternoon. John had taken the *ayahuasca* and sat waiting, cross-legged, next to her. Although I had said I wasn't going to "take care of anyone" that night, saying that to myself and Carolyn allowed me to see the difference between enabling an addict—my wonderful, alcoholic mother—and actually supporting my friends.

In the smoky, candlelit darkness, I walked over to the log where Stuart and Peter were sitting and sat down between them. "If you guys need to find me to talk tonight, please do," I said, saying what I, myself, would have wanted to hear. Who knows if that's what they needed, although each of them nodded warmly. After a while I left them. Each was in his own experience. I rejoined Carolyn and John. I felt alert as an antenna and calm in that expectant circle.

The shamans sat together in front of the fire in the center of the room. They chanted quietly. From somewhere I can't explain, inside or outside the lodge, I heard water flowing, perhaps from the string of an instrument—a beautiful, uncanny wavering, not like a Jew's harp exactly, yet noticeable, like a voice breaking through the veil of sleep. I wasn't sure if it was being made by one of the shamans, yet it seemed to come from another world, like a stream flowing inside a cave. I wanted to find words for something that had no comparison. I drifted on that sound in my own dugout canoe, in a current taking me where I needed to go, wherever I could see the song.

Across the room, Macarena headed for the door. The *ayahuasca* had taken hold of her. Was *Arutum,* her vision, arriving? Others walked out, too. They puked in the bushes. It was hard for me not to laugh. Perhaps it was the familiarity of the noise or the embarrassment at overhearing what usually is private. I wasn't puking, yet neither was I approached by the spirit as my friends were.

I remembered my college freshmen dormitory and too many weekend nights when my classmates and I, drunk and unguided, puked our guts out, having almost poisoned ourselves with whiskey and beer. The only guides we had were a few upperclassmen, trying to persuade us, as drunk as we were, to pledge their fraternities.

Suddenly, Lucho, who had been assigned by Daniel to watch any of us who wandered into the jungle, carried something—somebody—through the door. He held a limp body in his arms. Daniel rushed to him. They both held a woman—it was Macarena—and carried her to a bed near the shamans. We had been told that the *ayahuasca* could cause low blood pressure. I don't know if I remembered that caution or if, in that moment, I was too terrified to feel scared. Somehow I knew Macarena would be cared for and revived. I sat there, stunned but calm. The shamans brought Macarena to a sitting position, and in the smoky darkness, brought her back to consciousness. She was okay. They had used their powers to actually "reduce" her dose of *ayahuasca* without touching her. I could have spent the rest of the night frightened and angry, but that lodge, the music, and our days together circled us with an invisible rope and tied us into life.

Carolyn and I decided to walk outside for some fresh air and to see what the others were doing. I did want to be helpful if I could, and at the same time I didn't want to be intrusive. The air was mild and washed in the floodlight of the moon. The grasses and trees were held in their own outlines. Everything in that illumination was brilliant—the named and unnamed, the known and unknown. Jane stood quietly to one side, looking at some plants. John was bent over, feeling his first wave of nausea.

Maria sat nearby—like Lucho, another non-drinker. They watched the seekers and shadowed them when it looked like they were heading too far into the jungle.

Without thinking, I put my arm around Carolyn's shoulder. She put her arm around my waist. Nothing seemed more natural. We stood there swaying like friends at a reunion, held by a past we had shared and never had together and held by watching the others in that pool of rainforest light. Three Shuar girls—perhaps eight or nine years old—watched us. They stood twenty yards away in the shadow of their lodge. They giggled when my gaze caught theirs. They pushed the youngest one in our direction. Carolyn waved the girl toward us.

Slowly she came forward. She stood with us for a long time and gazed up into our faces as if we were the night sky. Occasionally she went back to her friends, then returned. More cautious of me, Marta fit into Carolyn's body like a daughter. Carolyn held her and filled some of the girl's emotional well. Later we learned that Marta, who was from another family, had been left to Martin by her mother. Her father had abused her. No one was sure what would happen to her. She was starved for nurturing. She let herself be held. Carolyn's embrace was her milk and honey.

After a while, Marta walked back to the other girls, who kept peeking at us as if they wanted to be held, too. Carolyn and I hugged each other. Standing there like the grass and trees in that striking light, we stood out and we blended in.

At times, drinkers emerged from the lodge as if called by the jungle. Stuart headed down the path toward a small clearing a few hundred yards away and looked around carefully. He, like Jane, had taken a second dose of *ayahuasca*, as the effect of one drink hadn't taken hold. I worried that, mesmerized or "called," he would take off into the forest.

"Stuart," I cautioned, trying not to sound too much like a principal, "that's good. Don't go any further."

"I'm fine," he yelled back, with an edge to his voice. He didn't want a watchdog.

With their flashlights, Lucho and Maria shadowed each person who came out of the lodge. I watched Stuart and tried not to appear to be monitoring him. Earlier, Peter had walked to the same place. I assumed he was seeing the Shuar's "real world" with his new eyes. Later, it seemed difficult for any of my friends to say exactly what their experience that night had been. They held it in their unique, personal containers.

John stepped out of the shadows. He had thrown up and was trembling, chilled with fear. He came over to Carolyn and I and we embraced him. I took off my sweater and wrapped it around his shoulders. He had tears in his eyes. Relieved, he said, "When I saw them carrying Macarena in, I was scared she was dead. I've been so worried we would lose someone. I'm so glad she's okay."

He let go of all he had been carrying, saying what I, and others, had felt at different times in our days in Ecuador. We, too, had been scared of dying and of being killed. We were glad for making it through the risks we had taken. I was relieved, too, by John's expression of the words I had been thinking and holding inside, however irrational they may have been. Warmed, John took a short walk on the path and returned, now delighted in what he was seeing and feeling. Carolyn and I walked back into the lodge. It was somewhere between midnight and two in the morning. People had begun to lie down and settle into their sleeping bags.

The shamans were in the middle of an intense healing. They attended to a neighbor, a woman who "had lost her ability to love"—depressed, we probably would say. She was furious at her husband, a shaman, who had taken another woman and put this curse on her. It sounded as if they were sucking the marrow from her bones and transfusing her with chant. There wouldn't be anything left of her, they were working so hard. Deep pain must need a powerful cure. From across the room I felt that she wouldn't be the same after that fierce attention, that washing of her spirit. I wouldn't be the same either.

When the shamans had finished her healing, they called Stuart and Peter. Each had his turn. The shamans sucked and sang their intrusions out and away. They rubbed herbs over their bodies. I floated over to them in my mind, part observer and part guardian angel, as if I were a medical student in a surgical amphitheater remembering the first time I saw into a body.

At sixteen, I worked as an orderly in the sprawling and bloody emergency rooms of Peter Bent Brigham Hospital in Boston, one of Harvard's teaching facilities. I wheeled people from ambulances and police cars through the swinging doors and to the curtained bays. A team of nurses, residents, and interns treated those patients, many of whom were drunk, beaten, and poor. I was amazed and shaken. I tried to be like the interns— cool and smart. A male athlete, and first-born, I, too, had learned to mask much of what I felt.

I walked the underground corridors, carrying charts and plastic bags of blood to the lab. The mystery and power of that vast building, the vulnerability of human beings, was palpable. In those basements, I passed old boiler rooms and laundries, laboratories, and graveyards of gurneys and iron lungs. I thought about death. I learned what happened to real people and what happened to their bodies. I stood in the back of the examining rooms longer than I was needed, as if I was a medical student. Is that how those interns first sparked their passion? They never kicked me out of those bloody classrooms.

One morning, an elderly African-American man was wheeled in. His left hand was wrapped in a rag. He had fallen from a loading platform and smashed his hand, and his knuckle had broken through his palm. No one was with him. He lived alone and had no family. The team cleaned his wound and told him he needed immediate surgery. They arranged for him to go to the operating room. He was bewildered and trusted them out of necessity.

It was Saturday. The hospital was understaffed. I was asked if I would take him upstairs and circulate as an OR orderly, where I would be in the surgical suite and retrieve things outside the room that might be needed. I felt close to this man by virtue of our mutual, yet different vulnerabilities. The surgeons repaired his hand and put the bones back in place under his skin. After he spent a few hours in the recovery room, I wheeled him back to his bed in the public ward. Groggy, he looked up at me with some recognition. I told him he was okay, and I would be back to see him.

Because of that work, I was transferred for the summer to the operating rooms to mop the floors and transport patients. Some of the first open heart surgeries and kidney transplants were performed in that city hospital. One morning, I held the ankle of an obese, diabetic woman as a resident prepped it for amputation. He painted it very slowly, and my hands trembled. Afraid I was going to drop her leg, I grabbed it where I shouldn't have touched and contaminated his work. He cursed me roundly and told me to do my part again—and do it right. This was the great, generous opportunity that came with working in a teaching hospital. Everybody made mistakes. Everyone was responsible for repairing what he or she did.

I visited this man, "my patient," twice. On the day of his discharge, I went back to say goodbye. He wasn't in his bed. Was he in the solarium smoking a cigarette? The nurse told me he had died in the middle of the night. He'd contracted a fast-killing virus. Was it possible he hadn't been asked the right questions about his immunizations? Had he been administered the wrong doses and shots? Someone I knew, however briefly, was dead and was not there anymore. He was a man with no family. He had died, I felt, for no good reason. My eyes swelled with tears, a grief of disillusionment. The world didn't work the way it was supposed to, but death did.

The shamans sitting across from me with their friends and relatives continued to chant, sing, and drink *chicha*. Through those late night and early morning hours, they voiced the same melody—a long love song. They punctuated each ending with a throaty *Hey*! The song was a stream, flowing its way through the center of Martin's house. I floated on their voices and the two vibrating strings of Charapa's violin. At one point, they rolled in laughter. Looking at Peter and his shiny bald head, they joked that they didn't know if they were seeing an elbow, a knee, or the polished top of a *chicha* bowl.

In the smoke and song, everyone found his place in that room. Carolyn and John lay down on either side of me. We said good night and fell asleep to some other waking, to a green and misty rainforest dream.

Traveling without one's spouse or partner can increase one's desire and ability to love. At the same time, it can create the possibility for a continued definition of a committed relationship. This was connected to the themes of our trip—fidelity to people, nature, and spirit, and commitment to things that are necessary and that matter.

The West's use and abuse of more than its share of the earth's resources, and the subsequent necessity of indigenous peoples to find quick, yet unsustainable ways to survive, are tied to concerns of the heart. What does it mean to be married, to be in a relationship with a partner and with the earth? In betraying another person, does it become easier to betray and destroy the earth—its plants and animals, water, dirt, and its spirit? Joseph Campbell wrote that in sacrificing something for a larger good, whether it is a relationship or the world, we create a sacred experience and the sacred.

As dawn approached, a hard, steady rain poured in the forest. I had heard about rains that lasted for days and stopped people in their tracks. Would we be held here by the weather and be unable to travel the next day? The Shuar found their beds and blew out the rest of the candles. After so many hours of drinking, I feared something would go out of control—something loud, something thrown, or someone hit.

I remembered drunken brawls in my college fraternity house. I recalled snowmobilers smashing bottles beneath my room one night in a lodge in Old Forge, New York. I didn't forget my mother's edginess after a drink. Nothing like that happened here. The singing and talking, the ritual and rain contained the intoxication. Even in consuming bowls of *chicha* during the course of a day and night, the Shuar did not expect each other to drink to drunkenness.

The room was completely black. Opening my eyes, I could see nothing in that darkness. Outside, creatures howled in the forest, near and far, far and near. Were they birds or cats? Maybe they were human sounds made by a war party. The Shuar were known for feuding, attacking in the middle of the night, and avenging a murder by taking an enemy's head. What about white heads? This was my only moment of pure terror in the jungle, in Ecuador, as if all of my accumulated anxiety was compressed into that image. I willed myself into a semblance of calm. I let the shrieks be a hoot, a call, and not a threatening human signal. I could live or die of fright. I relaxed in that choice, in the steady breathing in that sleeping room.

I don't know if I dreamt, dozed, or drifted in a sleepless canoe.

Suddenly, I sat up and looked out into the dark room. I saw my face inside the face of a disembodied jungle cat, possibly a jaguar's, a face that appeared to be a crowned sun. It was just there, gazing at me beyond my own fixed stare. I shuddered in my sleeping bag. I was afraid I was hallucinating. I worried that I had been dosed with *ayahuasca* in my canteen and that I had inhaled a spiked smoke—the old "contact high." I was fearful of going crazy and losing control. As I had many times in the mountains and in the jungle, I saw the choice my fear offered me: to panic or to be with what was.

I looked back at my animal self—that image. I took it in. I didn't run toward or away from it. Part of me emanated from its face. At the same time, it was its own visage. There was nothing more to do but be here in the darkness together. Many spirits were evoked in that room, from the jungle around us. This human jaguar was one appearance, one visitation. My belief was based on what I experienced. I became more curious and captivated than scared as the spirit brightened and faded, and as I breathed easily in my body.

The Shuar believe that *Arutum*—soul power—arrives in the form of two jaguars or anacondas fighting one another near the seeker, and that a person can appear in the image of a disembodied head or a ball of fire rolling through the forest. In seeing that image, the spirit explodes and later is transformed into an ancestor, an old man, who tells the seeker he has the blessing of a long life, the power to kill and be protected from his enemies, to be strong, wise, and honorable. In that moment, I knew I could live together with that flowering, fiery man-cat—the co-existent human, animal, and plant worlds. I could live in and with my vision in that room. I could say what I saw and what I felt.

Did I sleep a minute or an hour? A woman in the Shuar's cooking room got up and stirred the new day's *chicha*. Most of us slept and shifted in our sleeping bags.

The rain stopped. Water dripped off the roof onto the ground. We needed to begin the day's journey back to Shell and eventually to Quito. It was unclear if we were going to have to hike two hours through the heavy mud back to Miazal and the airstrip. Daniel thought the Shuar might be able to pole their canoes up river to us if the waters weren't too strong after the night's rain. I lay on my pack inside Martin's smoky house, completely exhausted and overwhelmed, thinking I had to carry myself through the jungle. Soul- and muscle-weary, I truly didn't know if I was going to make it or if I was going to get home. Daniel, always aware and intuitive, looked to me and asked, "Are you okay, my friend?" I answered by asking him if we were going to have to hike back. I felt like a third grader who couldn't take another step.

"You'll be fine," he said. "The canoes are coming." Daniel had a way of helping each of us keep moving beyond our limited view of ourselves.

He had a way of gently expecting compliance and accomplishment, even if we didn't trust our own competencies. No one was going to fail, be left behind, or die. Everyone would be changed.

As the sun rose and sliced through the staves of the walls, the women and girls, nine or ten of them, gathered in a semicircle, a Shuar choir. In their language, they sang us a song of farewell—the grandmothers and aunts, mothers and daughters. They smiled through their strong and broken teeth. As we had with the Quechua by the crater lake after receiving their music, we formed our chorus and sang the songs we could sing back, songs we knew by heart. We sang *Take Me out to the Ball Game* and our anthem, *Amazing Grace.* The Indians lowered their heads as if they were in a church. Love passed between us and beyond melody. We gave ourselves to each other.

Martin stood between the two shamans, holding his hunter's blowgun. He motioned to us to step outside with him. He told Daniel, in Spanish, that he wanted to show us how he used his weapon, his tool. In the sunlight, he set up a target in the wet grass—a squash on a stake at twenty yards. Chickens pecked around it. The girls walked in and out of its range. Martin took a dart from his pouch, spun some poisonless cotton around the tip, and inserted it in the hardwood pipe's end closest to his mouth. He lifted the weighty, eight foot blowgun, and in a quick, strong, effortless breath, blew the small arrow to its target. The first one just missed. The second one quivered into the soft plant as if it pierced a heart. The Shuar use these long killing instruments to drop a monkey, a bird, and in former days, an enemy.

Martin handed his blowgun to Peter and Stuart and eventually to me. With his strength, holding his elbows close to his body, he could hold the gun straight and steady. To create leverage, I had to extend my arms completely, holding the blowgun in front of me like a minuteman's long rifle. I blew and nothing happened. In my next breath, the dart looped out a few yards into the mud. Martin inserted another dart. I steadied the blowgun and in a perfectly unpracticed *whoosh*, I blew the Q-tippy arrow into the left side of the target. I screamed with delight. My yell was mirrored by the cagy smile on Martin's face. There's nothing like hitting the bull's-eye in the jungle in front of your oldest male friends, in view of women, and in the company of a warrior!

We needed to begin our long day of travel and to walk to the river to see if the Shuar had been able to negotiate the roiling water. Carolyn embraced Marta, the abused girl. Daniel said goodbye to his *compadre* Martin. We each shook hands with our hosts, the shamans, our new friends. We gave away what we had to give, shirts and other supplies. I handed Martin my son's Swiss army knife—the one he had been given for his Bar Mitzvah. I had borrowed it for the trip. My son would appreciate my leaving it in the rainforest and giving it to this Shuar father.

We walked single-file on the muddy path through the forest and down toward the river, away from Martin's house, away from the smoke and its dreamy, watery songs. On the other side of the log bridge, Peter slipped and scraped his leg. He fell into the mud, a dirt that would glaze him all day. He turned right as I kept going toward where I thought the others had gone. Within seconds we were separated. Peter was out of sight and sound. I called ahead for the others to stop where they were until we could reel him in. John said he would go after him and took off in the other direction.

The tall grasses brushed my legs. How easily a rookie in the jungle could walk away forever and disappear into a swirling compass. I could lose my friend. I heard John call out in the bush. Finally, Peter shouted back. He had wandered beyond a planted corn field, actually not that far off. Anyone not in sight was far away and lost. Tethered again, he walked with John and me to the others, who had found the river and were waiting for the Shuar's canoes. We stood there among the viny trees and plants, the men in one group and the women in another. Whatever pulled us together at times also moved us into our private selves. Our talk was small. We were still held in the ceremony of our night at Martin's lodge as we said goodbye to the jungle and anticipated saying goodbye to each other.

The evening deluge had left the air steamy. Cities of insects swarmed around us and raised welts on our arms and backs. I kept looking down river for the canoes. The water was wild. It could take a while for the Shuar to pole upstream. Air Amazonas, our flight back to Shell, expected to meet us before noon. In Ecuador, waiting was another way of being where you are, quieting expectation, and talking with a companion.

Still exhausted and knowing we were leaving, I felt edgy, as if I were stranded at an airport, my plane circling, delayed in the clouds. A canoe poled into sight and eventually tacked its way over to us. Daniel asked who wanted to leave on the first trip. Selfishly, I was ready to get going and loaded my pack into the canoe with Nancy, Stuart, and Daniel. In the stern, Mariano pushed us off into the fast water. We were leaving; we were going back.

Mariano's deaf-mute brother, Angel, stood in the bow. From time to time, Mariano struck his straight oar on the side of the boat to get his brother's attention. We rocked in the turbulent river and took some water into the canoe. It was my job to sit and do nothing. Twenty minutes down river, the waves were whitecapped. The canoe veered away from some rocks and listed to its left.

Daniel must have seen or felt something he didn't like. He pointed and told Mariano to steer the canoe into a sandy low spot in the middle of the river's converging currents. We climbed out, hung onto the gunwales, and bailed water with our hands. Fatigued, Daniel looked concerned. Taking my signal from him, I felt my own anxiety rise. I stepped back into the canoe and looked across the river to where we needed to go, as if by looking clearly, I could do my share of navigating and poling.

We headed into the fast water. Daniel pointed and shouted. Mariano struck his pole against the boat to signal his brother. We rolled, but not all the way over, and came through another pounding heartbeat into a smoother stretch of water. Whenever I thought we were done with challenges, a new one presented itself, saying, *Here's what needs to be done now.*

Mariano steered to an opening in the river bank where another canoe had been dragged up. We slid and scraped onto the shore and unloaded ourselves and our packs. An engine droned nearby. We slipped up the embankment and walked a few hundred yards, our last walk in the jungle.

We emerged at the edge of the airfield, where the red and white plane idled. The pilot waved to us to hurry. He had three trips to make with our group and wanted to make sure we flew in a window of good weather; there was no time to linger. In that hustling moment, I felt an overwhelming gratitude, an unspoken closeness with Mariano, who had met us when we arrived, who had put us into teams on the basketball court, and who had taken us swimming in his river—the same man who had led us to the thermal falls and to Martin's house, and had now brought us to the airstrip.

A few days earlier, Mariano had admired my sports watch with its flashing digital numbers. I unclasped the watch and handed it to him, hoping he would feel the affection I felt. I didn't know what else to do. He smiled and, looking at me, he looked into me. He shook my hand with his wild orchid's, warrior strength.

We hurried onto the plane and waved goodbye. The Cessna sprayed mud down the grass field and lifted off. We rose off the jungle floor as quickly as we had nosed down four days earlier. The cooler air rushed through the plastic vents. Everything that had happened, that I saw, heard, and felt, was below me, in my mind, and in my spirit.

No one said anything on the flight back to Shell. The dispatcher's voice strained through the static of the plane's two-way radio. Tears came into my eyes. Mist hit the windshield as we sheered through the bigger clouds. I felt deeply sad leaving the Shuar, Helmut, Patrice, and Maria, the living and disappearing forest, and the part of myself I found walking in the jungle and sleeping by the river. My eyes welled up with tears of relief, the wish to return, and the dread of not knowing what would remain of the rainforest and the Shuar.

Hernando, our pilot, veered the plane to the left. The big river swirled in the basin below. Swatches of cut jungle, like an unplanned quilt, stood out next to the colonists' houses and sheds. The main street and military buildings of Shell appeared in front us. Hernando made his approach close to a long ridge. A plane's wings and struts reflected up from below as trash in the trees. We glided onto the runway road, touched down, and taxied into our other lives. Even Daniel let out a yell as we came to a stop by the cinder block hangar. We unloaded quickly so the plane could circle back a second time for the others and make a third trip for our gear. Dazed, we piled into the van and drove down the street to the checkpoint to retrieve our passports.

Daniel walked through the chain-link gate of the military base, across the concrete yard, and into a brown one-story building. Five minutes later he emerged, obviously distressed, shaken, and seething. The officer who held our passports was away from his desk for the afternoon. He was at a party in the mountains for one of his colleagues. If we wanted to leave Shell that afternoon, we would have to drive an hour to find him, hopefully sober and cooperative. Daniel bullied the van through the dust and broken streets, pointing north out of town. He had been up most of the night—most of all the nights. Even this pacific man was over-tired and angry. We sped the first half-hour and stopped for gas, where I bought sodas for us. Daniel laughed when he saw the bottles. "Did they say anything when you took them with you?" he queried me. Even if the owner had said something in Spanish, I wouldn't have known what he meant. "No one takes bottles in Ecuador. It's too expensive. We'll stop and drop them off on our way back." What other local customs was I blind to?

In Puyo, Daniel took Stuart, Nancy, and me to a small hotel for lunch. The innkeeper greeted Daniel warmly by name. We ate quietly, shocked by the shift of location from the jungle and the unspoken realization of where we had been and what we had left. The street was loud and busy. News droned on a television. Daniel disappeared inside a newspaper. We finished a big meal, no one having to fast in preparation for *ayahuasca*, and thanked the owner on our way out. Antsy, we pushed on toward the resort where the officers' party was taking place.

The road took us off pavement and onto dirt and wound into the hills. I prepared myself for having to spend a night in a dark room in Shell, and for another chance to practice dealing with what presented itself rather than the way I wished things to be. I was pleased when Daniel found the officer and he pleasantly agreed to ride back with us to his office to return

our passports. I had no idea how much Daniel had paid for his coopera-
tion. On the way back, to the amusement of the mechanic at the gas station, we stopped to return our soda bottles.

As we drove into Shell, I was relieved to see the rest of our group. They
had just landed, and they were walking the sidewalk looking for us. We ate
again in the same small restaurant we had eaten in four days earlier. Peter,
in his t-shirt and shorts, was still slicked with mud from his slip on our
hike out of the jungle. We talked without listening to each other. There was
too much happening inside us. We were beginning to go home.

After lunch, we waited another few hours for the pilot to have his meal
and make the trip to Miazal to retrieve our packs. We strolled. We sat by
the street, talked a bit, and watched the cars and people as we tried out
the pan flutes and drums we had with us. Being in each other's company
buffered the change, our sadness, and kept us from caring too much about
the long ride to Quito that lay ahead.

Restless, I walked near the striped gate at the military checkpoint. The
soldiers were teenagers. They looked like kids with a summer job. This
was their work and their post. When a car stopped for clearance, the local
children swarmed it, selling drinks and cakes. Next to their stand, a monkey—the only monkey I saw in Ecuador—made a jungle gym of its cage.

The afternoon ended like a shade being slowly drawn down. Air
Amazonas pulled up to the chain-link fence next to the dispatcher's office.
To our surprise, Helmut and Patrice stepped out of the tiny plane door.
Helmut was dressed in the same t-shirt and cotton pants he'd worn in
Miazal. He flashed his endearing smile. They were greeted by Patrice's
sister Ester, who was bringing her husband's body back to the jungle. We
were only a few hours from saying goodbye, and there was great joy among
us in this runway reunion.

We had a five-hour drive to Quito in front of us. Daniel herded us
into the van. We were losing light and had to make our way back over the
Andes. I settled into my seat and leaned against the glass like a camper
busing home after a long canoe trip. Daniel wound us up that paved and
dirt road. The ravines and river fell behind us. Trucks and buses veered
toward us, and twice Daniel carefully backed up into a ditch to make
room for an unhappy driver to get by us. We drove through a few towns,

settlements really, where everyone was in the streets, talking and milling around, ending their day. Our van turned a few heads and became more dust in the air. We traveled—a movie in reverse—over the rainforest side of that mountain. Primary jungle and carved-out patches of colonist logging reappeared. In the darkness, we were shuttling to the other side of the moon.

In Baños, Daniel slowed and asked a man where we could buy music. He took us to his own apartment. We wanted new tapes to sing us back to Quito.

Daniel pushed that van as hard as he could over the miles of those hours—nine, ten, eleven o'clock. Sometimes he shimmied near the unguarded edge. Sometimes he drifted over the center line. He was tired, and from time to time he asked for the trago bottle. "A small drink will keep me awake," he said. Behind him, we looked at each other. Jane tried to distract him from drinking. For some reason, no one, not even the therapists and recovering people among us, drew a line with Daniel. No one said, "No way, *amigo*." Perhaps, after having climbed to the thermal falls and hiked to Martin's house, we gave ourselves over to the myth of our invincibility and Daniel's magical protection. Still, I did not want to die in a van wreck, so we took turns talking to keep Daniel awake with our jokes.

An hour from Quito, Daniel stopped for gas. Salsa blasted from the tape deck. Spontaneously, we danced in the aisle of the van, struck our drums, and shook our maracas and Shuar shell belts. The van rocked and rolled from side to side. Two men, sitting in their car behind us, looked astonished and pleased. *Gringos going crazy* was the title of that song.

Weaving to nine thousand feet, we saw the lights of Quito flickering below. It was near midnight, and the city was lit with its own fallen stars. We talked Daniel awake and down into the city. Tired, buzzed, and maybe a bit in love with us, he sang and danced at the steering wheel. He loved our letting loose. He was back in another of his Ecuadorian homes.

We were hungry. Daniel took us to an all-night restaurant in El Oro Verde, one of the fanciest hotels in Quito. Our city selves turned on. We behaved like urbanites under those soft-lit chandeliers, amid the late-night, after-theater crowd. Our hearts were still in the rainforest. A man and his wife, leaving the hotel, came over to our table and greeted Daniel.

They were friends of his from Cuenca. There was no one, it seemed, who didn't know him and for whom he didn't have a few words.

I was overwhelmed by the menu, by having to choose from so many things, by realizing the journey we had made and the gulf between cultures and ways of life. In one day we had hiked through the jungle mud and poled in canoes down the fast waters of Rio Mangosiza. We'd flown over the jungle canopy and driven up and over the Andes and down into the traffic of the city. With each change in place and mode of transportation, we'd left part of ourselves behind, taken what we needed, and gained our changing hearts and minds. How had we gone from the jungle in the morning to gold-handled electric doors in Quito in the evening? How had we held both experiences, so they could inform and imagine the other? Exhausted, I felt baffled and delighted by those multiple realities, the swirl of competing and complementary lives. It was our world of concrete and palm leaves, wire and vine, stories and dreams.

A couple sitting next to us said we looked like characters who had stepped out of a cartoon. Muddy, unshaven, wild-eyed, we were living in two cultures—jungle and city. We ached for bed. We paid our bill and giddily danced out the door. Peter still wore his muddy t-shirt and nylon running shorts. By pretending not to care what other people thought, we tried to postpone re-entry, being back, and going home. Perhaps we were masking our self-consciousness and our guilt at what we could choose to see and what we could have at the earth's expense.

We drove Lucho home before returning to the Hotel Ambassador. As we had for Umberto, we pooled some money to give him as a token of appreciation for his good cooking and his watchful presence. He was tearful in his gratitude to us. In his neighborhood in Quito, Lucho had been badly beaten and robbed, and was still recovering. His jaw was partially wired. As he walked off toward his family's apartment, he kept looking back and waving.

At almost two o'clock in the morning, we turned into the hotel's driveway. A wedding party had just ended. The guests danced out and greeted us with their celebration. I dragged myself up the stairs in that thin air, to the room Stuart and I shared. I don't remember falling asleep. I don't remember sleeping. A bird called in Miazal. A truck took a corner in Quito on two wheels.

Stuart and I woke up almost at the same time. I looked over and saw his sleepy, bearded, smiling face. How many times in high school, in college, in our long friendship, had we acknowledged the pleasure of a shared experience? We got up, showered, and called our wives in New England. In the jungle we had been virtually unreachable, although Don Juan's two-way radio could have patched a message through Shell to Quito and to an international operator. There was no radio at Martin's house, only singing and dreaming. Speaking to my wife was a way to tell her and myself I was safe; I had walked through the jungle. I was saying goodbye to Ecuador. I was coming home.

The Hotel Ambassador's dining room was noisy. A number of couples and groups were eating their first meal in Quito and beginning their journeys. They had their Ecuador days in front of them. Perhaps I did, too, in a future trip and in the writing of our story.

Daniel, showered and surprisingly refreshed, joined John, Peter, and me. We talked about the ongoing projects we had imagined—ways to stay connected to the people, land, and visions of Miazal, ways we could help preserve that part of the forest and the Shuar culture—with their direction. Daniel continued to be more enthusiastic than he had been initially at the kitchen table at Helmut and Patrice's house. He saw beyond our moment of goodwill, that we wanted to make a commitment to our values and to his. We would not abandon our words.

I shared my idea for a name for our work and our group. It was a name to keep us connected to each other, to our experience, to the Shuar's rainforest, and to our hopes: *Manos a Miazal*—Hands to Miazal. Each word was important, particularly *to*, which communicated to Daniel and to us that we walked the same earth, respectfully, in partnership.

I had forgotten how good Ecuadorian breakfast tasted—coffee with warm milk, glazed breakfast rolls, and fresh *naranjilla* fruit juice. Daniel had another full day—our last—planned and unplanned for us. His good friend, Enrique, a former teacher, joined us to guide us through the city. He told us the stories of the buildings, the people, and the coming election and its implications. Ecuador was about to vote itself back to the democratic right with the hope that Sixto, a former mayor who had once lived in Boston, could reduce bureaucracy. The people hoped his government could provide better access to human services, particularly medical care, improve a desperate economy, and support the Indians' land claims.

We climbed into the van one more time and drove through the heavy morning traffic. Enrique, standing in front, shared his story of Quito and of the monuments and buildings we passed. I heard only some of what he said. I was still in the dream and ceremony at Martin's house, in our hiking, canoeing, flying, and riding. I felt sad that I didn't listen to everything Enrique said. He was a good teacher. He wanted us to understand what we saw and how we could go from the living mud of the jungle one day to the dead concrete the next.

The streets were crowded with rush-hour traffic. The poor hawked things at stoplights. The disabled slept on the sidewalks next to their crutches and upturned hats. This could have been almost any city, coughing itself up in the exhaust of another day.

A year before, walking near Grand Central Station in New York, I had passed a row of boxes in a doorway. One of them moved. A man's legs extended out. The rest of his body was covered by the roof of his box. He was asleep or dead inside. Up and down the street there were many boxes. A cardboard village housed the homeless. I remembered this as Enrique translated the painted slogans about the upcoming election smeared across a storefront. Ecuador needed to shed its bureaucracy, so people could have access to services. How we mirrored ourselves across the hemispheres!

We drove by a few restored castles, ornate haciendas planted between office buildings, and into the city's hills. The *Nacional Militario*, where we had picked up our maps before heading to see the shamans, overlooked the commercial areas on one side and on the other, a valley where artists lived. The great painter, Oswaldo Guayasamin, resided in view of a battlefield. We stopped briefly in front of the Congress to admire the flag, the national seal, and the dramatic frieze around the building that portrayed the country's history. No Shuar here. The Indians organized their own independent federation from which to speak and exert their power.

A few blocks away, Daniel found an impossible parking place near the President's Palace. He told the traffic cop we were anthropologists, weary from our recent work, and asked us to limp out of the van. That tale, or the anticipated tip of *sucres*, allowed us a parking spot half in the street, half on the sidewalk. On the way to the square, Enrique led us through the spectacular Church of San Francisco, a great cathedral adorned in painting and statuary, in gold and silver leaf. A winged Jesus hovered over the chancel. On whose backs were these riches made? The Church knew and the bishop near Miazal, who cut back funds to the Mission, knew, too.

As we left, Enrique pointed out a middle-aged man and his mother walking to one of the chapels. "That's Felipe. Once he fought for the world boxing championship. He's one of our great heroes. I see him here often." A man in his bruised body prayed in this wooden and stone house of God.

We walked to the President's Palace through a street loaded with vendors. Daniel and Enrique impressed on us the danger from pickpockets. They wanted us to stay together and to keep our pockets flat. Other than my moment of terror two nights before at Martin's in the jungle, this was the first time I felt threatened by the familiar and by the possibility of random violence. Growing up in Boston, I rode the buses and subways and worked at my father's pool room and bowling alley in what was known on Washington Street as the "Combat Zone." I still had some street sense, even after living in Vermont, and yet, after feeling trusting in the Ecuadorian countryside and in the rainforest, I felt saddened by this other reality of having to be cautious and self-protective.

Nothing dangerous happened to us that morning. We walked across the square and up the stairs of the palace, past the expressionless, ceremonial guards standing with their bayoneted rifles. Daniel wanted us to see Guayasamin's murals. This time he fabricated the story that we were art historians. The security colonel, chief of the president's own force, told us to come back in fifteen minutes. They were clearing the corridor, as *el Presidente* was about to leave the building. We left and never returned. Enrique had many places he wished to show us and stories he wanted to share. With pride in his country and love for his friend, Daniel, he wanted to do the most he could with us. The two men were recent friends. John said Enrique, too, was a shaman.

Our hours in Ecuador were numbered. We wanted to buy things to bring home for family, friends, and a few mementos for ourselves. We split up and shopped the stores for brightly colored sweaters, hand-strung necklaces, and sparkling salsa dance tapes. I bought more than my suitcase and duffle bag could hold. Daniel stopped outside a hardware store, so Stuart and I could buy plastic tubing to put our Shuar spears in for the flight home. I didn't know if airport security would reject those "weapons" and cut off the parrot feathers adorning the grips. Once, when I was driving back to Vermont from Nova Scotia, custom officials snipped the owl feathers from a Micmac headdress I had bought. This brought my son to tears. I understood protection for endangered species, but not the protocol of border patrol.

The work day was over and traffic was heavy again. We promised ourselves a last evening of dining and dancing. Trago and affection would keep us together for a few more hours in Ecuador. At the hotel, I took a shower and stayed awake past the nap my body craved. We planned to meet for a few minutes before we went out again to present a gift to Daniel, to acknowledge and confirm our time together, and to share what was in our hearts.

We gathered in an alcove next to the hotel lobby. Drinks were ordered, and we sat, clean and dressy, and slid—a little too quickly—into artificial social chatter. In the morning, I had left my muddy jungle clothes to be washed, and they were still being dried. I sat, out of fashion, with my friends, waiting for a clean shirt and a long pair of pants. They arrived, and I changed. Like seniors the night before graduation, we snapped pictures as if we hadn't clicked hundreds of images, including many of each other.

Peter stood and invited Daniel to stand with him. It was new to see Daniel sheepish and not leading, about to receive our love and praise. As always, Peter spoke from his heart. Daniel had been our father, brother, guide, and *compadre*. We knew how deeply he cared for his country, the Shuar, and the complex environmental, political, and spiritual issues facing us all. Peter told him of our appreciation for his commitment and for his friendship. For taking us into his world and into our own conscience. For helping us see more clearly what our immediate choices were. For helping us take the next, necessary step. As the newly formed and named *Manos a Miazal*, in Daniel's honor we committed ourselves to sending funds to support the education of Shuar children and the purchasing by the Shuar of their own rainforest. We would find ways to share our experience in our lives at home and to bring new students to the hearts of Ecuador to tell others what we had imagined and felt and the songs we had seen. We would be conscious of our own excesses.

Daniel was visibly moved. We went beyond our roles and into the shared hemisphere of human love. I had one other presentation to make before we headed into the city. In Vermont, I'd stashed a few gifts in my suitcase, including a stack of colorful bandanas printed with Holstein cows, designed by Middlebury artist Woody Jackson. Early on in our trip, it became clear that the clearing of land to graze cows in the jungle was one of the great destroyers of primary forest and one of Daniel's furies and regrets. I had kept those bandanas imprinted with cows to myself. While the cow was appearing in Ecuador—the people needed to have something to eat, or sell so they could eat—the dairy cow was disappearing from pastures in Vermont. Like most images, the figures on these cloths meant something different to each of us. They spoke in two languages, in each cultural reality.

We had gained enough trust in one another to understand our good intentions. With Daniel watching, I gave bandanas to Macarena, Jane, Carolyn, and Nancy. Together we came to learn the many meanings of what we saw. We learned to see differently and to see beyond our own perspective. Finally, I reached behind me and held up my hiking boots. "Here, Daniel, these are for you," I said. "You told me how hard it was for you to find shoes your size in Ecuador. Thanks for letting me step where you have walked." We embraced, two Jews in Quito, brothers for another night, with mud in our spirits and salsa on our minds. We stepped into the cool city air and into the van. Nancy's eighty-year-old mother rejoined us. She had stayed at the hacienda in Otavalo while we flew into the rainforest. An adventurer at heart and a psychologist by craft, she was delighted to be included in our last night's fiesta.

We were late for our dinner reservations, but Daniel and Enrique still wanted us to see an old section of Quito and to take us up the winding road to the city's spectacular lookout, El Panecillo, where we could feel as if we were flying in the Andes again. Turn by turn, the city spun out below us, a holiday of lights. Quito sparkled.

We passed around the trago we had presented to Daniel and toasted each other, Ecuador and the gods infusing the heights. Daniel didn't want us to get out of the van. "It's more dangerous than you think," he warned. Yet he stepped out for a cigarette and a view as familiar to him as his skin. As if we had been sung to—and we had been—we were moved to sing *Amazing Grace* in gratitude to Daniel and Enrique, to the spirit among us, and to *la noche*.

We drove back down the mountain to La Rotunda, a traditional Ecuadorian restaurant. It was after nine. The Otavalan musicians played their guitars, drums, and pan flutes. We continued to say goodbye and to pack this journey into our memories. Jane was happy. She bargained for an Indian drum with one of the players. She could keep the heart of this trip beating at home in Miami. We finished, closed the restaurant, dropped Nancy and her mother back at the hotel, and then, like milers sprinting their last hundred yards, we urged ourselves to a few more hours out in the city. We stretched this night toward dawn and our flight home.

Daniel drove us to a salsa club. He was greeted by the owner as a dear friend. She was an old lover. Their romance appeared to offer a memory of gratitude. The bar had alcoves of tables and three squares for dancing. The Quito couples merengued themselves into braids. *Sex with clothes on*, I thought, delighting in the strong beat, sharp trumpets, and the confidence in their dance. Daniel, Enrique, and Macarena danced in the comfort and pleasure of being in their own neighborhood. The rest of us danced, too. We imitated them and tried to dance through the self-consciousness that a pitcher of beer could erase.

A dance is embracing and letting go of a partner at the same time. All the music of our journey mingled here—the chanting of the shamans, the drumming and fluting of the Quechuas, the singing of the Shuar, and the salsa of the radio. No doubt Daniel could have danced us from the club to the airport. Part of me wanted to stay, to will myself through my fatigue and stretch this night into another week. But we needed a few hours to finish packing, to sleep, and to dream ourselves away.

Around two in the morning, we left Enrique at his car and returned to the hotel. I found my room at the Ambassador and slept in the half-sleep of anticipating the alarm. In that two-hour instant, the telephone rang; Stuart and I awoke. We carried our bags down to the lobby, where everyone else had dragged themselves. A shower wasn't the same as a good night's sleep. We loaded the van one last time. Daniel drove us through the Quito streets. Night shaded into dawn.

International flights bring people together earlier than necessary and sooner than they are ready. We sleep-walked through baggage and passport checkpoints, knowing and denying we were leaving, saying goodbye to Daniel and the music, the rainforest, and the dream that met in his soul—the soul of Ecuador—that had met and joined ours.

Daniel had guided people through his country for nine years, and had driven them to the airport for almost a decade. There is no professional goodbye. He embraced each of us and stood by a far wall smoking a cigarette as we disappeared from his sight. I imagined him turning back to the doors opening to the street and turning us back to our lives—to do what needed to be done, to see the songs we could sing.

POSTSCRIPT

Dear Reader,

I have been remembering and writing the story of this journey for many years. The past has become the present. In each revision, I continue to see where I have been, with whom I traveled, walking in the Andes, hiking in the rainforest. Ever more clearly. Ever more cherished. I hear the songs I saw, the shamans who sang them.

I had difficulty with the text's tenses. Fact wanted to become poetry. Poetry needed to become fact. I felt like I was dreaming in order to remember and writing in order to speak.

I needed to write and re-write each sentence. I needed to have someone else check my work, to put one word in front of the other. I needed to keep going back, to see who is there and what remains.

> *I am afraid we are losing the worlds of our earth.*
> *I am not afraid to weep when I can. To stand in the way.*
> *I am not a government, a company.*
> *I cast one vote across the river.*
> *I bury fear's blindfold.*
> *I walk across the bridge.*

Gary Margolis
Cornwall, VT
June 2012

Gary Margolis, Ph.D, is Executive Director of College
Mental Health Services Emeritus and Associate Professor
of English and American Literatures (part-time) at
Middlebury College. He was a Robert Frost and Arthur
Vining Davis Fellow and has taught at the University of
Tennessee, University of Vermont, and Bread Loaf Writers'
Conferences. His third book, *Fire in the Orchard,* was
nominated for the 2002 Pulitzer Prize in Poetry. His poem
"The Interview" was featured on National Public Radio's
"The Story." Boston's Channel 5 interviewed him on the
Middlebury College campus reading his poem "Winning
the Lunar Eclipse" after the 2004 World Series.

Dr. Margolis was awarded the first Sam Dietzel Award
for Mental Health Practice in Vermont by the Clinical
Psychology Department of Saint Michael's College. His
clinical articles have appeared in the *Journal of American
College Health Association, Adolescence,* the *Ladies' Home
Journal,* and *Runner's World Magazine,* and he has been
interviewed on his work with college students by *Time
Magazine* and CBS News.

Gary Margolis lives with his wife, Wendy Lynch,
in Cornwall, Vermont. He can be contacted at
margolis@middlebury.edu.

A Flâneur/Peripatetic Production

Deep travel engages the mind as much as it does the body, contributing toward what might be referred to as an "active intellect". Whether strolling about a city or engaging in discussions while venturing into the countryside, Flâneur/Peripatetic Productions are devoted to exploring those roads, within and without, that are truly less travelled.

GREEN FRIGATE BOOKS

"THERE IS NO FRIGATE LIKE A BOOK"

Words on the page have the power to transport us, and in the process, transform us. Such journeys can be far reaching, traversing the landscapes of the external world and that within, as well as the timescapes of the past, present and future.

Green Frigate Books is a small publishing house offering a vehicle—a ship—for those seeking to conceptually sail and explore the horizons of the natural and built environments, and the relations of humans within them. Our goal is to reach an educated lay readership by producing works that fall in the cracks between those offered by traditional academic and popular presses.

RELATED FLÂNEUR/PERIPATETIC PRODUCTIONS TITLES

A Wanderer All My Days:
John Muir in New England

J. Parker Huber

Ultreia! Onward Progress of the Pilgrim

Robert L. France

Westward I Go Free:
Tracing Thoreau's Last Journey

Corinne Hosfeld Smith